AF644389

ARCHAEOLOGICAL SITES OF SOUTH PANCALA

Data from Archaeological and Literary Sources

ARCHAEOLOGICAL SITES OF SOUTH PANCALA

Data from Archaeological and Literary Sources

ANNAMARIA DALLAPORTA
LUCIO MARCATO

MANOHAR
2005

First published 2005

© Authors, 2005

All rights reserved. No part of this publication may be reproduced or transmitted, in any form or by any means, without prior permission of the authors and the publisher

ISBN 81-7304-636-0

Published by

Ajay Kumar Jain for
Manohar Publishers & Distributors
4753/23 Ansari Road, Daryaganj
New Delhi 110 002

Typeset at

Digigrafics
New Delhi 110 049

Printed at

Lordson Publishers Pvt Ltd
Delhi 110 007

Distributed in South Asia by

FOUNDATION BOOKS

4381/4, Ansari Road
Daryaganj, New Delhi 110 002
and its branches at Mumbai, Hyderabad,
Bangalore, Chennai, Kolkata

In memory of
Shri Hazarimull Banthia

CONTENTS

PREFACE

For some years now, our studies have focused on the ancient kingdom of South Pancala.

This interest we owe to our friend, late Shri Hazarimull Banthia (Kanpur, UP), enthusiastic about and committed to all possible ways of revealing, developing and enhancing the historical and archaeological potential of the site of Kampil. His contagious enthusiasm stimulated us to carry out numerous studies in the field over the years. Our aim was to shed light on the vicissitudes of South Pancala during the first millennium BC, starting with the first of many questions: had Kampil really been the capital of the kingdom?

This question rested on a contradiction: in 1887 A. Cunningham had identified Kampilya, the capital which, according to literature, had origins prior to the tenth century BC, with the village of Kampil; on the basis of the exploratory diggings carried out in 1976, however, the latter appears to have originated in the seventh century BC.

Our discussions at the Banaras Hindu University (1996) reinforced the doubts on the validity of Cunningham's hypothesis and therefore, taking action, we decided to study the territory at both the local level (10 km around Kampil) and the regional level (South Pancala), using literature, remote sensing techniques and simple exploration, in an attempt to reconstruct the environmental and cultural context of Kampil. After an initial series of surveys, at 6 km from Kampil we discovered (with other Italian scholars) the site of Drupad Qila which in many respects still remains a mystery (Dallaporta, Marcato 2001).

Its baked brick boundary walls, the almost exactly rectangular layout and the fairly large dimensions (830 × 680 m), make this site particularly interesting, providing fresh stimuli and posing new questions.

In the meantime we had gathered all the information available in archaeological literature on many more or less extensive sites of all ages. Sometimes they were only brief indications, whereas at other times they were reports, not always exhaustive, of surveys and, even more rarely, accounts of excavations; each was important because it helped to define the general picture of the sequence of archaeological situations that had occurred over time. Having only very few direct data, it was essential to collect all the indirect data that could have even the slightest bearing on the subject. In this way we compiled over 700 file cards which we believe will be useful to scholars interested in the archaeology of South Pancala.

Our intention is to display the archaeological information contained in the file cards on a geographical basis, thus combining time and space in an archaeological map which provides an effective work tool not only for archaeologists but for all those in some way responsible for the administration, protection and valorization of the territory. These file cards constitute the first step and provide the descriptive part with respect to the map itself, which is more symbolic and direct. We also hope that the data collected here can be integrated and enriched with data from possible detailed surveys of the territory, such as those recently conducted by Dr. Dhilip Chakrabarti (Cambridge University) in some districts of the valley of the Ganga (Chakrabarti 2001).

The principle we have used is to follow the most common transliteration accepted in the International Archaeological literature and to exclude all diacritical marks.

At the moment, however, as a first step, we would be interested to hear from scholars who wish to send us any corrections or data missing from our file cards or other data on new sites for updated editions of this collection.

ANNAMARIA DALLAPORTA
LUCIO MARCATO

THE SITES OF SOUTH PANCALA

The Land of Pancala

In literature the borders of South Pancala are described very approximately; the uncertainty of the indications and the difficulty of reconciling them with the territory as it is today mean that many compromises, perhaps debatable, have to be made in establishing their location. It has been agreed that South Pancala comprised the modern districts of Uttar Pradesh: Bulandshahr, Aligarh, Etah, Mainpuri, Etawah, Farrukhabad and Kanpur. In some of these districts, probably not all the area was actually part of South Pancala, but for the sake of convenience we refer to the present administrative units, in their entirety, aware that the ancient borders could not have been either linear or static.

The territory examined is very uniform, with a typical large river plain morphology. The alluvium has constructed a micro-elevation, the maximum difference in level (a few metres) of which is found on the edges of an earlier fluvial terrace where, strategically, various settlements grew up in the Iron Age, exploiting the proximity of the river and the slightly raised position. Remote sensing furthermore enabled us to identify intense fluvial dynamics documented by traces of numerous paleo-riverbeds testifying to the deviations, also in recent times, of the Ganga, Yamuna and their tributaries.

As regards the Ganga, its gradual shift from south-west to north-east means that it is now located a few kilometres away with respect to the situation approximately three thousand years ago (Iron Age) on ground which has perhaps dropped in level following neotectonic phenomena which, between the middle of the second and the beginning of the first millennium BC, also modified the hydrographic system of the Indus.

The Ganga with its floods and deviations, has been and continues to be the main morphogenetic agent: man has adapted to its moods, defending himself from them and at the same time benefiting, instilling, as often happens in these cases, both fear and gratitude at a religious level.

The Yamuna is associated with a very special river: according to Hindu tradition, where it flows into the Ganga, at Prayag (Allahabad), one of the most sacred rivers, the Saraswati, 'mother of all rivers' also joins up, following an (improbable) underground path. This hypothetical confluence (*trivedi sangam*) of religious significance perhaps recalls the former documented influx of the Yamuna into the Saraswati, the course of which coincides, at least partly, with that of the river Ghaggar. The subsequent deviation of the Yamuna to the east to meet the Ganga and similar movement in the opposite direction of the Sutlej which occurred at some time between 1400 and 1000 BC, led to a decisive reduction in the volume of water of the Saraswati which, at a certain point along its course, ran dry and became absorbed by the sand (Gupta 1995; 155).

Up to the beginning of the Bronze Age, the territory was probably covered by a more or less dense undergrowth (jungle), the extent of which was progressively reduced by the increasing demands of agriculture and animal rearing. Comparison between the data obtained from archaeology and data extrapolated from literature identifies a process of technological and demographic development from the sixth century BC that had obvious effects on the environmental behaviour and the techniques of exploitation of natural resources.

Information on the rural society of Mauryan India can be obtained from Buddhist literature and especially from the *Arthasastra*, although the latter describes ideal situations, often far removed from day-to-day reality. Although some significant changes have definitely taken place in the administrative system and in the morphology of the territory over the centuries due to causes attributable to both man and nature, little has changed overall, especially in the life of the villages, thus favouring the continuation of cultural and behavioural patterns that have been reflected in many structural characteristics of the environment.

Pancala: Historical-literary summary

From ancient literature we know that the territory of Pancala, after the ninth century BC, stretched from the foothills of the Himalayas to the river Yamuna to the south, surrounded by other *mahajanapadas* such as the Kuru to the north-west, the Kosala and the Videha to the east.

Between the fourth and the second millennium BC, the region was covered by thick vegetation with extensive marsh along the rivers: human settlement, which had begun more than 3,000 years previously, gradually modified the original environment. Only traces of the latter remain and are confined to the hilly area to the north.

The sources are fairly inaccurate and at variance as regards both the names of the clans that formed Pancala and their number (Shrimali 1983, 25) with a repeated preference for the number five (in Hindi: *panc*, in Sanskrit: *pancan*), also exploited on other occasions, perhaps suggesting, rather naively, an improbable origin of the term 'Pancala'. Thus, according to the Puranic legends, the first king had five sons who governed five provinces which could coincide, according to vague indications in literature, with the division of the region according to the cardinal directions, in addition to a central part.

Around the fourteenth century BC, a mixed set of groups of various origin settled in the region, then known as Pancala, mixing with the more or less autochthonous local population and expressing a homogeneous culture which, benefiting from a favourable economic and technological situation, considerably boosted general development. In a few centuries, the tribal type society was transformed into a more sophisticated organization based on a consolidated agricultural economy which constituted a basis for the formation of the *mahajanapadas* (structurally similar to the kingdoms).

On several occasions the Pancala tribe (which gave its name to the territory) was seen as closely connected with that of the Kurus, even becoming one single *raja* for a certain period.

The Puranas talk about Ajamidha, the forefather of three dynasties of rulers: the Pauravas (Kurus), the Bharatas and the Ajamidhas (the last two governed North and South Pancala respectively) (Shrimali 1983, 30). This genealogical reconstruction, more of a legend than a historical document, also underlines the strong link that characterized the alliance between Kurus and Pancalas, to which a common origin was attributed. Despite this, inevitable tensions deteriorated relations several times to the point of erupting into open hostility causing alternating supremacy over the region and therefore its division (perhaps around the ninth century BC) with the Kurus to the north-west of the territory.

The tacit existence of the reign of South Pancala appears to become evident in the eleventh century BC (with King Nipa), merging after just two centuries with the events of the North which, subsequently, it frequently joined up with and separated from, although how and when is not yet clear.

Very little in history is final, especially in India: from the *Jatakas* it appears that some *rajas* of South Pancala resided at Ahichchatra (capital of the North) and vice versa. In other words it appears that, to further complicate the situation, at some time in the history of the two Pancalas, they were not clearly separate.

With the conquest of the Nandas (325 BC), Pancala's fate was governed by that of the successive empires (Maurya, Sunga, Kushan, Gupta) and kingdoms, enjoying two brief periods of independence: the first from the middle of the second century BC to the end of the first century AD, during which it experienced a non-monarchical government; then between the end of the Kushan empire and the beginning of the Gupta empire (AD 300-350).

In the sixth century AD, the whole of the Doab was conquered and taken from the Guptas by Harivarman of Maukharis, who established the capital at Kanauj (Farrukhabad district). King Harsa was a member of the powerful Maukhari family and was an important personality whose actions, recorded in epigraphy, were narrated and highlighted in literature.

In the eighth century AD, supremacy over the Doab was disputed by various parties, but the struggle was won by a clan of the Gurjara tribe, the Pratiharas, originating in Central Asia, who extended their control over most of northern India, maintaining Kanauj as their capital. An epigraph (on a stone slab) found at Jhinjauta (a mound outside the perimeter of the walls of Drupad Qila, 6 km from Kampil, Farrukhabad district), carrying the name of Raja Bhoja (AD 836-850) which says he wanted a temple on the site dedicated to Vishnu.

The sovereignty of the Gurjara-Pratiharas lasted from AD 810 to 1036; after the incursions of Mahmud of Gazni, they abandoned the field briefly to the Rastrakutas and then, in 1085 AD, to the Gahadavalas who resisted the increasingly frequent pressures of the Islamic armies until the end of the twelfth century AD.

All this is taken from literature and history; at the moment archaeology has too few data for comparison and verification.

The excavations carried out, and the identification and recognition of a number of sites are certainly not sufficient to outline a reliable picture of the overall situation, but they are fairly significant for identifying the following cultural aspects, not rigidly consecutive (Shrimali 1983, 36):

a. Possible links with and references to the civilization of the Indo-Saraswati; seventeenth-eleventh century BC.

From the seventeenth to the fourteenth century BC only the presence of Harappan ware is documented which from the fourteenth to the eleventh century BC is associated with Ochre Coloured Pottery (OCP).
From exploration of the territory it emerges that a network of settlements existed spaced at distances of 8-12 km.

b. OCP cultural complex; twentieth-sixteenth century BC (with fairly flexible limits).
Epicentre located in the district of Saharanpur (upper Doab). The settlements were generally small (approx. 200 × 200 m) and were inhabited for short periods.

c. Phenomenon of the copper hoards.
The numerous finds of copper artefacts, often similar and grouped (maybe hidden) in hoards, scattered all over the Doab but concentrated in South Pancala (the phenomenon must be extended to the whole of India, however) have been interpreted as the expression of a particular cultural attitude even though opinions on this are conflicting.
Association of the copper hoards with the OCP also appears far-fetched: only their pre-Painted Grey Ware (PGW) dating is plausible.

d. Black and Red Ware (BRW) cultural complex.
In the excavations of Atranjikhera, another class of pottery, the BRW, dated 570 BC, emerged between the OCP and PGW levels.
At Jakhera the P. I is characterized by BRW which re-appears, after a pause, in the second part of the P. II together with PGW.
At Hastinapura (Meerut district), at the borders of Pancala, the situation of the BRW is different again as it appears together with PGW.
As can be seen, at the moment it is not possible to identify a stable coherent presence of BRW in the region although it is attributed a specific cultural contribution.

e. PGW and Northern Black Polished Ware (NBPW) cultural complexes; iron technology.
PGW appears to characterize the first two phases of the Iron Age in particular and is commonly considered an expression of the population of the Mahabharata.
The NBPW was identified by J. Marshall (1911-12) who interpreted it incorrectly; for some time it was considered a

subsequent autonomous cultural expression with respect to PGW.

Many scholars are currently inclined to consider the two classes of pottery, the first more widespread in the upper valley of the Ganga and the other more concentrated in the middle part, as different phases of one single culture (Roy 1986, 5).

File Cards and Data

For compilation of the file cards of the archaeological sites of South Pancala, we had to rely on data from many varied sources, often the cause of differences in assessment and terminology. During processing, all information that was too vague from the topographical point of view was discarded (such as data without co-ordinates and indication of the district), since it was impossible to personally check all doubtful information. Despite this, in a certain number of file cards the data are sparse, incomplete or approximate, but we considered even limited information to be important in a situation characterized by endemic lack of data.

If credit has been given to the fairly reliable indications at geographical level, some caution must be exercised as regards chronology if dating has been performed more than a few decades ago or in any case without the use of tested scientific methods.

Optimal data are obviously those that we have been able to check, on which ancient literature and archaeology agree and of whose dates we are absolutely certain.

In our case we are decidedly nowhere near this ideal situation which, realistically speaking, is still a long way off.

It should be pointed out that the data provided in the file cards do not refer only to the periods of existence of South Pancala but concern all archeologically significant aspects of the territory, up to the twelfth century AD (and also later, in cases in which it seemed important to underline continued use of the site), thus recording situations and changes over a long period of time.

Reading of the File Cards

The file cards are ordered per district, in alphabetical and numerical order. At the end of the collection, a general index will facilitate the search for individual sites.

The information grille summarises very concisely the data necessary for pinpointing the site geographically and archaeologically. Each datum provided will be accompanied in the file card by the bibliographic reference from which it has been taken.

All the sites have been included in the grille, independently of the possibility of completing them in all parts with the data in our possession. The missing information can be entered personally by anyone who has the information because these data file cards are designed as a work tool: with use, they can be completed and extended to make them more efficient especially if linked to the archaeological map of the region which we hope to produce shortly.

The information grille consists of the following items in succession, indicated in the file cards by their respective initials (highlighted here in bold type):

No. [Progressive number (per district)]	Name of the site
Localization	Geographical co-ordinates; district; *tahsil* and geographical indications in general.
Type of site or remains	Form and consistency of the site, e.g. mound, settlement, fort or indications of structural remains such as wells, tombs, walls or temples.
Chronology, Period, Culture	Information concerning the age of the site, at times very approximate and cursory, especially in the case of survey indications (tendency to make cultures and pottery classes generally coincide or to assign an age time interval that is too long).
Description of finds Location of Finds	Characteristics of the various most frequent or most significant types of finds (artefacts and structures) identified on the site. Place of conservation of the finds described above.

References	Books, articles and personal communications from which the information contained in the file card has been obtained.
Notes	Special notes on the site and the data specified. A question mark (?) indicates that the author is not certain about the information he has provided.

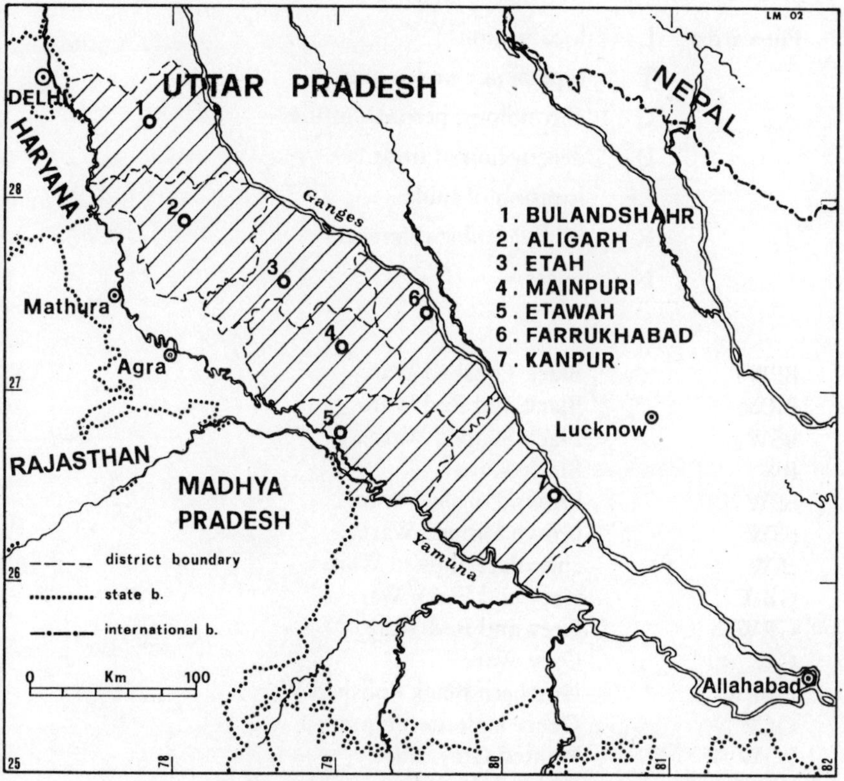

The cross-hatched area indicates very approximately the territory of the ancient kingdom of South Pancala.

ABBREVIATIONS

File cards:	L	localization
	T	type of site or remains
	C	chronology, period, culture
	D	description of finds
	LF	location of finds
	R	bibliographic references
	N	notes

BPW	Black Polished Ware
BRW	Black and Red Ware
BSW	Black Slipped Ware
BW	Black Ware
bPW	brown Polished Ware
bSW	brown Slipped Ware
cSW	chocolate Slipped Ware
GBW	Grey and Black Ware
GRW	Grey and Red Ware
GW	Grey Ware
NBPW	Northern Black Polished Ware
OCP	Ochre Coloured Pottery
PGW	Painted Grey Ware
RPW	Red Polished Ware
RSW	Red Slipped Ware
RW	Red Ware
c.	*circa*
circumf.	circumference
cult.	culture
d.	diameter
P.	chronological period (if dynastic: period)
N, S, E, W, etc.	cardinal directions

ALIGARH DISTRICT

40 Sites

1. Andos	
L	
T	
C	Early Historical P.
D	Finds not described
LF	
R	*IAR* 1962-3, 31 Ghosh 1989, vol. 2, 20
N	

2. Astmadi or Nagla Astal	
L	*Tahsil* Hathras
T	Temple
C	Tenth century AD
D	Brick temple in ruins
LF	
R	*IAR* 1990-1, 69
N	

3. Bajhera	
L	
T	Mound

C	PGW cult.
D	Sherds
LF	
R	*IAR* 1962-3, 31 Shrimali 1983, vol. I, 196 Ghosh 1989, vol. 2, 42
N	

4. Bergaon	
L	*Tahsil* Hathras
T	
C	*c.* Tenth century AD
D	Remains not described
LF	
R	*IAR* 1990-1, 69
N	

5. Bharatpur	
L	
T	Mound
C	PGW cult.
D	Sherds: PGW, BRW
LF	
R	*IAR* 1962-3, 31 Shrimali 1983, vol. I, 196 Ghosh 1989, vol. 2, 66
N	

6. Bhogaon	
L	*Tahsil* Hathras
T	
C	*c.* Tenth century AD
D	Sculptures
LF	Scattered in the village
R	*IAR* 1990-1, 69
N	

7. Chintapur	
L	*Tahsil* Hathras
T	Mound
C	Late Historical P.
D	Sherds: RW
LF	
R	*IAR* 1990-1, 69
N	

8. Chursiarn or Turseen	
L	*Tahsil* Hathras
T	
C	Tenth century AD
D	Sculptures
LF	Scattered in the village
R	*IAR* 1990-1, 69
N	

9. Gangauli–Nagla Katta	
L	*Tahsil* Hathras
T	
C	Tenth century AD
D	Sculptures
LF	Scattered in the village
R	*IAR* 1990-1, 69
N	

10. Gangchauli	
L	*Tahsil* Hathras
T	
C	Tenth century AD
D	Sculptures
LF	Scattered in the village
R	*IAR* 1990-1, 69
N	

11. Gohan Khera	
L	
T	
C	Early Historical P.
D	Finds not described
LF	
R	*IAR* 1962-3, 31 Ghosh 1989, vol. 2, 152
N	

12. Hathras Fort	
L	*Tahsil* Hathras H.Q.
T	Mound
C	PGW cult., NBPW cult., Sunga-Kushan period, Late Historical P.
D	Sherds: PGW, GW, NBPW, BSW, BRW, RW (Sunga-Kushan), others (?)
LF	
R	*IAR* 1954-5, 61 *IAR* 1966-7, 33 Shrimali 1983, vol. I, 197 Ghosh 1989, vol. 2, 167
N	

13. Jafrabad	
L	*Tahsil* Hathras
T	
C	Tenth-Eleventh century AD
D	Sculptures Architectural remains
LF	Scattered in the village
R	*IAR* 1990-1, 69
N	

14. Kaithora	
L	
T	

C	PGW cult.
D	Sherds
LF	
R	Tripathi 1976, 127
N	

15. Kalwa	
L	
T	
C	Early Historical P.
D	Finds not described
LF	
R	*IAR* 1962-3, 31 Ghosh 1989, vol. 2, 197
N	

16. Kauriaganj	
L	Mound on the right bank of the Kali River Field 450 m E of mound
T	Mound: 50 × 100 m, 3 m high
C	OCP cult., PGW cult., Sunga-Kushan period
D	• Mound: Sherds: PGW, GW, BSW, BRW, RW (Sunga-Kushan) • Field: Sherds: OCP

LF	
R	*IAR* 1965-6, 84 Ghosh 1989, vol. 2, 211
N	

17. Kharva	
L	*Tahsil* Hathras
T	
C	Tenth century AD
D	Sculptures
LF	Scattered in the village
R	*IAR* 1990-1, 69
N	

18. Khera	
L	*Tahsil* Koil
T	
C	PGW cult., NBPW cult.
D	Sherds: PGW, NBPW
LF	
R	*IAR* 1962-3, 70 Shrimali 1983, vol. I, 198 Roy 1986, xiv Ghosh 1989, vol. 2, 226
N	

19. Khera Chaturbhuj (sub village of Sikandarpur)	
L	*Tahsil* Hathras
T	Mound
C	Late Historical P.
D	Sherds: RW
LF	
R	*IAR* 1990-1, 69
N	

20. Khera-Teh Koil	
L	
T	
C	PGW cult.
D	Sherds
LF	
R	Tripathi 1976, 128
N	

21. Koka	
L	*Tahsil* Hathras
T	
C	Tenth century AD
D	Sculptures
LF	Sattered in the village
R	*IAR* 1990-1, 69
N	

22. Komri	
L	
T	Mound
C	PGW cult.
D	Sherds
LF	
R	*IAR* 1962-3, 31 Shrimali 1983, vol. I, 199 Ghosh 1989, vol. 2, 233
N	

23. Kumarai	
L	*Tahsil* Hathras
T	
C	Tenth century AD
D	Sculptures
LF	Scattered in the village
R	*IAR* 1990-1, 69
N	

24. Lakhnau	
L	
T	
C	Early Historical P.
D	Finds not described
LF	

R	*IAR* 1962-3, 31 Ghosh 1989, vol. 2, 250
N	

25. Madrak	
L	*Tahsil* Kol
T	
C	NBPW cult.
D	Sherds: NBPW, GW, BSW
LF	
R	*IAR* 1966-7, 33 Shrimali 1983, vol. I, 199 Ghosh 1989, vol. 2, 263
N	

26. Mahawa	
L	*Tahsil* Iglas
T	
C	Early Historical P., Late Historical P.
D	Sherds: NBPW, BSW, GW, others (?)
LF	
R	*IAR* 1966-7, 33 Shrimali 1983, vol. I, 199 Ghosh 1989, vol. 2, 264
N	

27. Maho	
L	*Tahsil* Hathras H.Q.
T	
C	PGW cult., Sunga-Kushan period, Late Historical P.
D	Sherds: PGW, BSW, GW, RW (Sunga-Kushan), others (?)
LF	
R	*IAR* 1966-7, 33 Shrimali 1983, vol. I, 199 Ghosh 1989, vol. 2, 268
N	

28. Majhola	
L	*Tahsil* Hathras
T	
C	Seventh-eighth century AD
D	Sculptures
LF	Scattered in the village
R	*IAR* 1990-1, 69
N	

29. Morthal	
L	*Tahsil* Kol
T	
C	OCP cult., PGW cult., NBPW cult., Sunga-Kushan period, Late Historical P.
D	Sherds: OCP, PGW, BRW, BSW, GW, NBPW, RW (Sunga-Kushan), others (?)

LF	
R	*IAR* 1966-7, 33 Dikshit 1979, 296 Shrimali 1983, vol. I, 199 Ghosh 1989, vol. 2, 293
N	

30. Nagaria Khera

L	*Tahsil* Sikandra Rao
T	
C	Late Historical P.
D	Remains not described
LF	
R	*IAR* 1966-7, 33
N	

31. Parsara

L	*Tahsil* Hathras
T	
C	Tenth century AD
D	Sculptures
LF	Scattered in the village
R	*IAR* 1990-1, 69
N	

32. Qila Hathras	
L	
T	
C	PGW cult., NBPW cult.
D	Sherds
LF	
R	*IAR* 1954-5, 61 Roy 1986, xiv Tripathi 1976, 129
N	

33. Saigarh	
L	*Tahsil* Sikandra Rao
T	
C	PGW cult., NBPW cult., Sunga-Kushan period, Late Historical P.
D	Sherds: PGW, BSW, GW, NBPW, RW (Sunga-Kushan), others (?)
LF	
R	*IAR* 1966-7, 33 Shrimali 1983, vol. I, 201 Ghosh 1989, vol. 2, 384
N	

34. Sankara	
L	32 km E of Atrauli
T	Mound: 1 × 0.5 km, 20 m high Fort

C	PGW cult., NBPW cult., Early Historical P., Late Historical P., Fifteenth-sixteenth century AD
D	Sculptures in red sandstone (Sunga-Kushan) • Mound: Sherds: PGW, NBPW, RW Terracottas (Sunga-Kushan, Gupta) Structural remains (ninth-twelfth century AD) • Fort in *lakhauri* bricks (fifteenth-sixteenth century AD)
LF	
R	*IAR* 1960-1, 32-3 Tripathi 1976, 31-2, 130 Shrimali 1983, vol. I, 201 Ghosh 1989, vol. 2, 391
N	

35. Sasni or Sasni ka Qila

L	
T	Mound
C	PGW cult., Sixth century BC to Late Historical P.
D	Finds not described
LF	
R	*IAR* 1962-3, 31 *BMA* 40, 61 Shrimali 1983, vol. I, 201 Ghosh 1989, vol. 2, 399
N	

36. Sherpur	
L	
T	
C	Early Historical P.
D	Finds not described
LF	
R	*IAR* 1962-3, 31 Ghosh 1989, vol. 2, 407
N	

37. Tappal	
L	
T	Mound
C	PGW cult.
D	Sherds
LF	
R	*IAR* 1962-3, 31 Shrimali 1983, vol. I, 202 Ghosh 1989, vol. 2, 431
N	

38. Tarfara	
L	
T	
C	Kushan period, Late Historical P.
D	Sherds: BSW, GW, RW (Kushan), others (?)

LF	
R	*IAR* 1981-2, 100
N	

39. Tuskan	
L	
T	Mound
C	PGW cult.
D	Sherds
LF	
R	*IAR* 1962-3, 31 Shrimali 1983, vol. I, 202 Ghosh 1989, vol. 2, 445
N	

40. Vijai Garh	
L	*Tahsil* Sikandra Rao
T	
C	PGW cult., NBPW cult., Late Historical P.
D	Sherds: PGW, BSW, GW, NBPW, others (?)
LF	
R	*IAR* 1966-7, 33 Shrimali 1983, vol. I, 202 Ghosh 1989, vol. 2, 462
N	

BULANDSHAHR DISTRICT

66 Sites

1. Acheja	
L	On the Kali-Nadi River
T	
C	PGW cult.
D	Sherds: PGW, GW
LF	
R	*IAR* 1959-60, 75 Tripathi 1976, 124 Shrimali 1983, vol. I, 195 Ghosh 1989, vol. 2, 1
N	

2. Ahar	
L	*Tahsil* Anupshahr
T	
C	Sunga-Kushan period, Late Historical P.
D	Sherds: GW, BSW, RW (Sunga-Kushan), others (?)
LF	
R	*IAR* 1970-1, 37 Shrimali 1983, vol. I, 195
N	

3. Ahmadgarh or Ahmadnagar	
L	*Tahsil* Khurja
T	
C	PGW cult., Sunga-Kushan period
D	Sherds: PGW, BRW, GW, BSW, GW, RW (Sunga-Kushan)
LF	
R	*IAR* 1970-1, 37 Tripathi 1976, 124 Ghosh 1989, vol. 2, 9
N	

4. Akrabas	
L	*Tahsil* Anupshahr
T	
C	OCP cult., Sunga-Kushan period, Late Historical P.
D	Sherds: OCP, RW (Sunga-Kushan), others (?)
LF	
R	*IAR* 1970-1, 37 Shrimali 1983, vol. I, 195 Ghosh 1989, vol. 2, 11
N	

5. Amanullahpur (Maharana)	
L	*Tahsil* Khurja
T	
C	NBPW cult.
D	Sherds

LF	
R	*IAR* 1965-6, 42 Shrimali 1983, vol. I, 195 Ghosh 1989, vol. 2, 15
N	

6. Asawar	
L	On the Kali-Nadi River
T	
C	PGW cult.
D	Sherds: PGW, GW
LF	
R	*IAR* 1959-60, 75 Shrimali 1983, vol. I, 196 Ghosh 1989, vol. 2, 24
N	

7. Astipur	
L	
T	
C	PGW cult.
D	Sherds
LF	
R	Tripathi 1976, 124
N	

8. Aurangabad	
L	
T	
C	Early Historical P., Late Historical P.
D	Finds not described
LF	
R	*IAR* 1963-4, 45 Ghosh 1989, vol. 2, 28
N	

9. Balai-kot	
L	
T	
C	PGW cult., Sunga-Kushan period
D	Sherds: PGW, GW, RW (Sunga-Kushan)
LF	
R	*IAR* 1964-5, 76 Tripathi 1976, 125 Shrimali 1983, vol. I, 196
N	

10. Barauli	
L	
T	
C	PGW cult.
D	Sherds

LF	
R	*IAR* 1964-5, 42 Tripathi 1976, 125 Shrimali 1983, vol. I, 196 Ghosh 1989, vol. 2, 53
N	

11. Bargaon	
L	*Tahsil* Khurja
T	
C	Early Historical P.
D	Sherds: GW, BSW, RW (Sunga-Kushan)
LF	
R	*IAR* 1965-6, 42 Ghosh 1989, vol. 2, 54
N	

12. Barner Sharif	
L	*Tahsil* Khurja
T	
C	PGW cult., NBPW cult., Sunga-Kushan period, Late Historical P.
D	Sherds: PGW, BRW, BSW, GW, NBPW, RW (Sunga-Kushan), others (?)
LF	
R	*IAR* 1966-7, 33 Shrimali 1983, vol. I, 196 Ghosh 1989, vol. 2, 55
N	

13. Bhangel-Begumpur	
L	
T	
C	Early Historical P., Late Historical P.
D	Finds not described
LF	
R	*IAR* 1963-4, 45 Ghosh 1989, vol. 2, 66
N	

14. Bhataola	
L	
T	
C	Early Historical P.
D	Finds not described
LF	
R	*IAR* 1962-3, 34 Ghosh 1989, vol. 2, 67
N	

15. Bhatpura or Bhatpur or Bhetpura	
L	
T	
C	OCP cult., PGW cult.
D	Sherds: OCP, PGW

LF	
R	*IAR* 1960-1, 66 Dikshit 1979, 296 Shrimali 1983, vol. I, 196 Ghosh 1989, vol. 2, 68
N	Some sherds of Harappa affinities

16. Bhogpur	
L	*Tahsil* Khurja
T	
C	PGW cult., Early Historical P., Late Historical P.
D	Finds not described
LF	
R	*IAR* 1963-4, 45 *IAR* 1965-6, 42 Tripathi 1976, 125 Shrimali 1983, vol. I, 196 Ghosh 1989, vol. 2, 74
N	

17. Birpur or Birupur	
L	On the bank of the Ganga
T	
C	PGW cult.
D	Sherds: PGW, GW
LF	

R	*IAR* 1959-60, 75 *IAR* 1962-3, 34 Tripathi 1976, 125 Shrimali 1983, vol. I, 196 Ghosh 1989, vol. 2, 79
N	

18. Biswana	
L	
T	
C	Early Historical P.
D	Finds not described
LF	
R	*IAR* 1962-3, 34
N	

19. Budhena	
L	*Tahsil* Khurja
T	
C	Early Historical P.
D	Sherds: GW, BSW, RW (Sunga-Kushan)
LF	
R	*IAR* 1965-6, 42 Ghosh 1989, vol. 2, 85
N	

20. Chandpur	
L	*Tahsil* Anupshahr
T	
C	OCP cult., PGW cult., Sunga-Kushan period
D	Sherds: OCP, PGW, RW (Sunga-Kushan)
LF	
R	*IAR* 1970-1, 37 Tripathi 1976, 125 Shrimali 1983, vol. I, 197 Ghosh 1989, vol. 2, 95
N	

21. Chipiyana	
L	
T	
C	Early Historical P., Late Historical P.
D	Finds not described
LF	
R	*IAR* 1963-4, 45 Ghosh 1989, vol. 2, 103
N	

22. Dadha	
L	
T	
C	Undated
D	Sherds: GW

LF	
R	*IAR* 1962-3, 34 Ghosh 1989, vol. 2, 110
N	

23. Dadri	
L	
T	
C	Early Historical P., Late Historical P.
D	Finds not described
LF	
R	*IAR* 1963-4, 45 Ghosh 1989, vol. 2, 111
N	

24. Danpur	
L	*Tahsil* Anupshahr
T	
C	Sunga-Kushan period, Late Historical P.
D	Sherds: RW (Sunga-Kushan), others (?)
LF	
R	*IAR* 1970-1, 37 Ghosh 1989, vol. 2, 115
N	

25. Darau	excavated
L	Opposite riverside of Durgam-Chundera
T	Mound
C	PGW cult., NBPW cult., Sunga-Kushan period, Late Historical P.
D	Sherds: PGW, NBPW, GW, BSW, others (?) Terracotta finds: animal figurines, gamesmen, wheels, beads, seal with *brahmi* characters Bone arrowheads Iron spearheads, nails Knife-handles Remains of structural activity (dwellings) (Sunga-Kushan)
LF	
R	*IAR* 1985-6, 78-9
N	Mound locally called Sidhpur

26. Dasehra	
L	
T	
C	Sunga-Kushan period
D	Sherds: RW
LF	
R	*IAR* 1964-5, 42 Ghosh 1989, vol. 2, 117
N	

27. Daulatpur	excavated
L	
T	
C	OCP cult.
D	Sherds: OCP Terracotta finds: balls, beads, wheels Stone objects: balls, weights, querns, pestles Remains of structural activity: post-holes, mud-clots, burnt patches, brickbats, plaster pieces
LF	
R	*IAR* 1984-5, 86-8
N	Affinity with the pottery of Lal Qila, Atranjikhera and Saipai

28. Deevlakhara or Deevla Khera	
L	*Tahsil* Anupshahr
T	
C	OCP cult., Late Historical P.
D	Sherds: OCP, others (?)
LF	
R	*IAR* 1970-1, 37 Shrimali 1983, vol. I, 197 Ghosh 1989, vol. 2, 118
N	

29. Dhaurau or Dhauran	
L	*Tahsil* Khurja
T	

C	PGW cult., Sunga-Kushan period, Late Historical P.
D	Sherds: PGW, BRW, RW (Sunga-Kushan), others (?)
LF	
R	*IAR* 1966-7, 33 Shrimali 1983, vol. I, 197 Ghosh 1989, vol. 2, 127
N	

30. Ghalibpur or Ghalipur	
L	On the bank of the Ganga
T	
C	PGW cult.
D	Sherds: PGW, GW
LF	
R	*IAR* 1959-60, 75 Tripathi 1976, 126 Shrimali 1983, vol. I, 197 Ghosh 1989, vol. 2, 145
N	

31. Ghatamwala	
L	
T	
C	PGW cult.
D	Sherds: PGW, GW
LF	

R	*IAR* 1959-60, 75 Tripathi 1976, 126 Shrimali 1983, vol. I, 197 Ghosh 1989, vol. 2, 146
N	

32. Ghazipur	
L	
T	
C	Early Historical P.
D	Finds not described
LF	
R	*IAR* 1962-3, 34 Ghosh 1989, vol. 2, 147
N	

33. Ghori-Bachchera	
L	
T	
C	Early Historical P., Late Historical P.
D	Finds not described
LF	
R	*IAR* 1963-4, 45 Ghosh 1989, vol. 2, 148
N	

34. Gujarpur	
L	
T	
C	Early Historical P., Late Historical P.
D	Finds not described
LF	
R	*IAR* 1963-4, 45 Ghosh 1989, vol. 2, 155
N	

35. Gulistanpur	
L	*Tahsil* Sikandrabad (Pargana Dadri)
T	Mound
C	Late Harappa P., PGW cult.
D	Sherds: Harappa pottery (western part), PGW (eastern part), GW
LF	
R	*IAR* 1963-4, 91 Shrimali 1983, vol. I, 197 Ghosh 1989, vol. 2, 156
N	

36. Hasangarh	
L	
T	
C	Sunga-Kushan period
D	Sherds: RW

LF	
R	*IAR* 1964-5, 42 Ghosh 1989, vol. 2, 164
N	

37. Indor	
L	
T	
C	Early Historical P.
D	Finds not described
LF	
R	Ghosh 1989, vol. 2, 175
N	

38. Ismailpur	
L	*Tahsil* Khurja
T	
C	Early Historical P.
D	Sherds: GW, BSW, RW (Sunga-Kushan)
LF	
R	*IAR* 1965-6, 42 Ghosh 1989, vol. 2, 176
N	

39. Jafarpur (Gurdipur)	
L	*Tahsil* Khurja
T	

C	Early Historical P.
D	Sherds: GW, BSW, RW (Sunga-Kushan)
LF	
R	*IAR* 1965-6, 42 Ghosh 1989, vol. 2, 179
N	

40. Janpat	
L	
T	
C	Early Historical P., Late Historical P.
D	Finds not described
LF	
R	*IAR* 1963-4, 45 Ghosh 1989, vol. 2, 183
N	

41. Jehra	
L	On the Kali-Nadi River
T	
C	PGW cult.
D	Sherds: PGW, GW
LF	
R	*IAR* 1959-60, 75 Tripathi 1976, 127 Shrimali 1983, vol. I, 198 Ghosh 1989, vol. 2, 184
N	

42. Katauri	
L	On the Kali-Nadi River
T	
C	PGW cult.
D	Sherds: PGW, GW
LF	
R	*IAR* 1959-60, 75 Tripathi 1976, 127 Shrimali 1983, vol. I, 198 Ghosh 1989, vol. 2, 210
N	

43. Khanpur	
L	
T	
C	OCP cult.
D	Sherds
LF	
R	Dikshit 1979, 296 Shrimali 1983, vol. I, 198
N	

44. Khurja	
L	
T	
C	PGW cult., Sunga-Kushan period, Late Historical P., Mughal period

D	Sherds: PGW, GW, RW (Sunga-Kushan), others (?) Epitaph (Mughal)
LF	
R	*IAR* 1964-5, 76 *IAR* 1984-5, 143 Ghosh 1989, vol. 2, 228
N	

45. Kiratpur	
L	
T	
C	OCP cult.
D	Sherds
LF	
R	Ghosh 1989, vol. 2, 229
N	

46. Kot	
L	
T	
C	Undated
D	Sherds: GW
LF	
R	*IAR* 1963-4, 45 Ghosh 1989, vol. 2, 236
N	

47. Kot-khera	
L	*Tahsil* Sikandarbad
T	
C	PGW cult., NBPW cult., Sunga-Kushan period, Late Historical P.
D	Sherds: PGW, BSW, GW, NBPW, RW (Sunga-Kushan), others (?)
LF	
R	*IAR* 1966-7, 33 Shrimali 1983, vol. I, 199 Ghosh 1989, vol. 2, 237
N	

48. Lal Qila	excavated
L	28°30′ N, 78°15′ E; *tahsil* Anupshahr; 24 km from Anupshahr
T	
C	OCP cult.
D	Sherds: OCP Copper finds: arrowheads, pendants, celts, etc. Terracotta finds: human figurines, beads, gamesmen, discs, etc. Other finds: carnelian beads, pestels, querns, bone objects, etc. Remains of structural activity: mud brichs, burnt bricks (27-30 × 20-23 × 7.5-10 cm), different floor levels, burnt patches (fire places ?)
LF	
R	*IAR* 1966-7, 33 *IAR* 1968-9, 35-7 *IAR* 1969-70, 38-40 *IAR* 1971-2, 45-6 Dikshit 1979, 287-8, 296

	Shrimali 1983, vol. I, 199 Possehl 1986, 59 Ghosh 1989, vol. 2, 251-3
N	C^{14} dates in: *IAR* 1969-70; Ghosh 1989 Affinity with the pottery of Atranjikhera and Saipai

49. Manpur	
L	W of the Ganga
T	
C	OCP cult.
D	Sherds: OCP Iron objects: celts, sward
LF	
R	*IAR* 1960-1, 66 Dikshit 1979, 296 Shrimali 1983, vol. I, 199 Ghosh 1989, vol. 2, 278
N	Some sherds of Harappa affinities

50. Nagla-ki-Rani	
L	
T	
C	Early Historical P., Late Historical P.
D	Finds not described
LF	
R	*IAR* 1963-4, 45 Ghosh 1989, vol. 2, 304
N	

51. Nizampur	
L	
T	
C	Undated
D	Sherds: GW
LF	
R	*IAR* 1962-3, 34 Ghosh 1989, vol. 2, 318
N	

52. Pindrawal	
L	*Tahsil* Khurja
T	
C	Sunga-Kushan period, Late Historical P.
D	Sherds: GW, BSW, RW (Sunga-Kushan), others (?)
LF	
R	*IAR* 1970-1, 37 Shrimali 1983, vol. I, 200 Ghosh 1989, vol. 2, 344
N	

53. Qawan	
L	
T	
C	Sunga-Kushan period
D	Sherds: RW

LF	
R	*IAR* 1964-5, 42 Ghosh 1989, vol. 2, 356
N	

54. Raipur	
L	On the Kali-Nadi River
T	
C	PGW cult.
D	Sherds: PGW, GW
LF	
R	*IAR* 1959-60, 75 Tripathi 1976, 129 Shrimali 1983, vol. I, 200 Ghosh 1989, vol. 2, 357
N	

55. Rasheedpur	
L	*Tahsil* Anupshahr
T	
C	Late Historical P.
D	Sherds
LF	
R	*IAR* 1970-1, 37
N	

56. Ronda	
L	
T	
C	Sunga-Kushan period
D	Sherds: RW
LF	
R	*IAR* 1964-5, 42 Ghosh 1989, vol. 2, 376
N	

57. Ruhullahpur	
L	
T	
C	Early Historical P., Late Historical P.
D	Finds not described
LF	
R	*IAR* 1963-4, 45 Ghosh 1989, vol. 2, 381
N	

58. Salempur	
L	*Tahsil* Khurja
T	
C	PGW cult.
D	Sherds
LF	

R	*IAR* 1965-6, 42 Tripathi 1976, 130 Shrimali 1983, vol. I, 201 Ghosh 1989, vol. 2, 385
N	

59. Salimgarh	
L	*Tahsil* Bulandshahr
T	
C	Late Historical P.
D	Sherds
LF	
R	*IAR* 1970-1, 37
N	

60. Shakoorganj	
L	*Tahsil* Anupshahr
T	
C	PGW cult., Sunga-Kushan period
D	Sherds: PGW, BRW, GW, BSW, RW (Sunga-Kushan)
LF	
R	*IAR* 1970-1, 37 Shrimali 1983, vol. I, 201 Ghosh 1989, vol. 2, 406
N	

61. Sonda-Jatpur	
L	*Tahsil* Khurja
T	
C	Early Historical P.
D	Sherds: GW, BSW, RW (Sunga-Kushan)
LF	
R	*IAR* 1965-6, 42 Ghosh 1989, vol. 2, 416
N	

62. Tajpur-Piaoli or Tajpur-Pioli	
L	
T	
C	PGW cult.
D	Sherds
LF	
R	*IAR* 1963-4, 45 Tripathi 1976, 130 Shrimali 1983, vol. I, 202 Ghosh 1989, vol. 2, 427
N	

63. Til-Begumpur	
L	
T	
C	Early Historical P.
D	Finds not described

LF	
R	*IAR* 1962-3, 34 Ghosh 1989, vol. 2, 439
N	

64. Usmanpur (Qila Mewi)	
L	
T	
C	Undated
D	Sherds: GW
LF	
R	*IAR* 1964-5, 42 Ghosh 1989, vol. 2, 453
N	

65. Utsera or Utsara	
L	On the Kali-Nadi River
T	
C	PGW cult.
D	Sherds: PGW, GW
LF	
R	*IAR* 1959-60, 75 Tripathi 1976, 131 Shrimali 1983, vol. I, 202 Ghosh 1989, vol. 2, 454
N	

66. Yeseenpur	
L	*Tahsil* Anupshahr
T	
C	PGW cult., Sunga-Kushan period
D	Sherds: PGW, GW, BSW, RW (Sunga-Kushan)
LF	
R	*IAR* 1970-1, 37 Tripathi 1976, 131 Shrimali 1983, vol. I, 202 Ghosh 1989, vol. 2, 469
N	

ETAH DISTRICT

177 Sites

1. Ajitnagar	
L	27°36′30″ N, 78°55′30″ E
T	Mound: 130 × 100 m, 7 m high
C	Late Historical P.
D	Sherds: GW Terracotta animal leg Metal blade
LF	
R	Singh 1979, 92
N	

2. Akbarpur Kot	
L	27°27′30‴ N, 79°09′ E
T	Mound: 80 × 60 m, 5 m high
C	Late Historical P.
D	Sherds Brickbats Ruined citadel (30 m^2) with towers at cardinal points
LF	
R	Singh 1979, 100
N	

3. Akbarpur Palia	
L	27°45′ N, 78°58′ E Mound, SE of village
T	Mound: 2 acres, 2 m high
C	Late Historical P.
D	Sherds: RW Sculptures Ruined plinth (*Sati* post ?)
LF	
R	Singh 1979, 96
N	

4. Arjunpur Qadim	
L	27°41′ N, 78°54′ E
T	Mound: 250 × 150 m, 15 m high
C	NBPW cult., Late Historical P.
D	Sherds: GW, BSW, BPW Terracotta object with stamped rosette Carved limestone pieces Bricks (39.5 × 26.5 × 9 cm) Mud-brick walls
LF	
R	Singh 1979, 91 Singh 1984 ?, 6
N	

5. Arora	
L	27°46′ N, 79°01′ E
T	Mound: 60 × 30 m, 1 m high
C	Late Historical P.
D	Sherds Limestone sculpture Brickbats
LF	Sculpture placed at the site
R	Singh 1979, 94
N	

6. Astipur	
L	
T	
C	PGW cult.
D	Sherds
LF	
R	Tripathi 1976, 124
N	

7. Atranjikhera	excavated
L	27°41′49″ N, 78°41′35″ E; right bank of the Kali-Nadi River
T	Settlement: 1600 × 400 m, 13 m high
C	OCP cult., PGW cult., NBPW cult., Early Historical P., Late Historical P., pre-Mughal period (?)

D	Sherds: OCP, BRW, PGW, BSW, GW, RSW, RW, NBPW, glazed pottery, Celadon pottery Terracotta finds: plaques, human and animal figurines, discs, beads, bangles and other objects Copper antimony rod Iron finds: arrow-heads, knives, chisels, hooks, fragments, etc. Copper finds: rings, bangles, hooks, chisels, fragments, etc. Coins (Kushan, indo-islamic) Seals (Gupta) Hindu sculptures (Gupta) Mud bricks and burnt bricks (33 × 22 × 6 cm) Remains of structural activity: dwellings, defences, granary, etc. Remains of a Jaina temple Other finds: carnelian, shell, glass beads and bangles; semiprecious stones; flakes of agate, chalcedony and bone
LF	
R	*AI* 1, 55 *AI* 10-11, 144 *IAR* 1960-1, 35 *IAR* 1961-2, 103 *IAR* 1962-3, 34-6 *IAR* 1963-4, 45-9 *IAR* 1965-6, 44-7, 91 *IAR* 1966-7, 72 *IAR* 1967-8, 45-6 *IAR* 1968-9, 37-8 *IAR* 1979-80, 75-6 Tripathi 1976, 24-5, 135, 136 Dikshit 1979, 126-7, 287, 296 Singh 1979, 24-6 Agrawal, Chakrabarti 1979, 384 Roy 1983, 26-7 Shrimali 1983, vol. I, 196 Singh 1984 ?, 1-2

	Possehl 1986, 10-11 Roy 1986, 37-8 Erdösi 1987, 2, 19 Ghosh 1989, vol. 2, 25-7 Chakrabarti 1997, 188-9 Chakrabarti et al. 2002, 116
N	Local tradition: capital of Raja Venu C^{14} dates in: *IAR* 1965-6; *IAR* 1966-7; Tripathi 1976; Agrawal, Chakrabarti 1979

8. Aun	
L	27°37′ N, 78°47′ E
T	Mound: 50 acres, 10 m high
C	Gurjara-Pratihara period
D	Sherds Hindu sculptures Brickbats, limestone and sandstone fragments
LF	A medieval sculpture is enshrined in a recent temple
R	Singh 1979, 61 Singh 1984 ?, 8
N	Local tradition: fort erected by Raja Venu

9. Aurangabad	
L	27°37′ N, 79°06′ E
T	Mound: 130 × 100 m, 5 m high
C	Late Historical P.
D	Sherds: GW, RW Sculptures Bricks (30.5 × 23 × 7.5 cm) Remains of foundation walls

LF	
R	Singh 1979, 97
N	A granary with charred grains found while digging (?)

10. Awagarh	
L	27°27′04″ N, 78°29′08″ E Fort erected on the mound
T	Mound: *c.* 20 acres Fort
C	PGW cult., Late Historical P.
D	• Mound: finds not described • Mud fort surrounded by a deep moat (circumf. 1 mile nearly)
LF	
R	Singh 1979, 102 Chakrabarti et al. 2002, 116
N	

11. Badhari	
L	27°45′ N, 78°37′ E
T	Mound: 100 × 80 m, 7 m high
C	Late Historical P.
D	Sherds: RW Hindu sculptures Bricks (35.5 × 18 × 5.5 cm)
LF	
R	Singh 1979, 81
N	Sherds painted or decorated

12. Badshahpur Loya	
L	27°35′ N, 78°45′ E
T	Mound: 8 acres, 9 m high Foundation wall (5 m^2)
C	Late Historical P.
D	Horizontal engraved beams • Mound: Sherds Hindu sculptures Bricks (25.5 × 26 × 6.5 cm) • Foundation walls maybe of an old temple
LF	
R	Singh 1979, 75
N	Gold coins and copper coins (?) found by villagers

13. Bahadur Nagla	
L	27°28′30″ N, 79°05′30″ E
T	Mound: 10 × 8 m, 2.5 m high
C	Late Historical P.
D	Sherds Hindu sculptural frieze
LF	
R	Singh 1979, 47
N	

14. Baheta	
L	27°47′ N, 78°45′ E Mound 1, W of village Mound 2, E of village Mound 3, S of village
T	Mound 1: 80 × 60 m, 1 m high Mound 2: 100 m², 1 m high Mound 3: 100 × 60 m, 1 m high
C	Late Historical P.
D	*Kankar* fragments • Mound 1: Sherds: BRW • Mound 2: Sherds: BRW, GW, painted pottery • Mound 3: Sherds: BRW, GW
LF	
R	Singh 1979, 82 Singh 1984 ?, 7
N	

15. Bahota	
L	27°42′30″ N, 78°55′ E
T	Mound: 160 × 100 m, 3 m high Well
C	Kushan period, Late Historical P.; Sultanate, Mughal periods
D	Terracotta human figurines (Kushan and later) Sculptures • Mound: Sherds: RW, GW • Well in *lakhauri* bricks (remains)

LF	
R	Singh 1979, 48
N	

16. Banail	
L	27°43′ N, 78°57′30″ E
T	Mound: 60 × 50 m, 2 m high
C	Late Historical P.
D	Sherds: RW, GW Terracotta beads
LF	
R	Singh 1979, 95
N	

18. Bania Dhera	
L	27°34′ N, 79°02′ E Mound 1, 1 km west of village Mound 2, east of mound 1 Mound 3, north-east of village Mound 4, east of village Mound 5, east of village
T	Mound 1: 160 m^2 Mound 2: 50 × 30 m, 2 m high Mound 3: d. 50 m, 5 m high Mound 4: d. 30 m, 2 m high Mound 5: 50 × 40 m, 2 m high
C	Late Historical P.

D	• Mound 1: Sherds Remains of a fort, 30 m^2, with towers, rampart in mud-bricks, burnt bricks and limestone fragments • Mound 2: Sherds Fragments of carved limestones Brickbats • Mound 3: Sherds Small replica of *stupa*, Buddhist images Brickbats and limestone fragments • Mound 4: Sherds Brickbats and limestone fragments • Mound 5: Sherds Brickbats
LF	Various sculptures collected in Saadatnagar village
R	Singh 1979, 68-9 Singh 1984 ?, 10
N	Mound 3: maybe a *stupa*

18. Bansa	
L	*Tahsil* Etah
T	
C	Late Historical P.
D	114 Hindu sculptures
LF	
R	*IAR* 1958-9, 74
N	

19. Baoli	
L	27°28′30″ N, 78°46′ E
T	Mound: 60 × 50 m, 5 m high Oval-shaped structure: d. 1.8 m, 3 m high
C	Late Historical P.
D	• Mound: Sherds • Oval-shaped structure (undated): Brick structure (worshipped by putting a brick on the top)
LF	
R	Singh 1979, 70
N	Oval-shaped structure: tomb of Bahlol Lodi (?)

20. Baragaon	
L	27°48′30″ N, 78°47′ E
T	Mound 1: 130 × 120 m, 2 m high Mound 2: 50 × 30 m, 2 m high
C	Late Historical P.
D	Sherds: RW, BW, GW Terracotta pestel and gamesmen
LF	Two medieval sculptures located at the site
R	Singh 1979, 84
N	

21. Barai	
L	27°39′ N, 78°32′ E
T	Mound: 100 m^2, 9 m high

C	Late Historical P.
D	Sherds Hindu sculptures 4 temple pillars Brickbats
LF	
R	Singh 1979, 76
N	

22. Barauna	
L	27°48′ N, 79°00′ E Mound, east of village
T	Mound: 1 acre, 2 m high
C	Late Historical P.
D	Sherds: RW Brickbats
LF	
R	Singh 1979, 96
N	

23. Bastarmau	
L	27°47′ N, 78°56′ E Mound adjacent to Burhi Ganga
T	Mound: 180 × 90 m, 22 m high Well
C	Late Historical P., Sultanate, Mughal periods

D	• Mound: Sherds: RW, BW, BPW, bPW, glazed ware Brickbats and *lakhauri* bricks Remains of foundation walls with mud-bricks and burnt bricks (30.5 × 23 × 7.5 cm) • Well constructed in bricks
LF	
R	Singh 1979, 93-4
N	

24. Basundhra	
L	27°28′30″ N, 78°32′ E
T	Mound 1: 50 × 16 m, 6 m high Mound 2: 60 × 30 m, 1 m high
C	Late Historical P.
D	Sherds Brickbats
LF	
R	Singh 1979, 71
N	Mound 1: a stronghold of Chauhans (?) Mound 2: locally called Harsinghpur

25. Bathawa or Bathwa	
L	27°29′ N, 78°32′ E
T	Mound: 120-30 × 50 m, 9-10 m high
C	Gurjara-Pratihara period

D	Sherds Hindu sculptures Wedge-shaped bricks (51 × 25.5 × 15 cm, 48 × 25.5 × 15 cm, 47.5 × 24 × 15 cm) probably employed in a round structure
LF	
R	Singh 1979, 81, 103-4
N	

26. Baunder

L	27°49′ N, 78°51′ E Mound 1, on the village Mound 2, north of village
T	Mound 1: 130 × 80 m, 10 m high Mound 2: 60 × 50 m, 2 m high
C	Late Historical P.
D	Sherds: painted and stamped RW, BW Terracotta conch
LF	
R	Singh 1979, 85
N	

27. Bausa

L	27°00′ N, 78°34′ E Mound 1, south of village Mound 2, north of village
T	Mounds (two) Temple
C	Late Historical P.

D	• Mound 1: Sherds Brickbats • Mound 2: Vestiges of towers (remains of a fort) • Temple (ruined): 172 terracotta figurines 114 Hindu, Buddhist sculptures Structural fragments
LF	Sculptures and terracottas collected in State Museum, Lakhnau
R	Singh 1979, 63 Singh 1984 ?, 6-7
N	

28. Bazidpur	
L	27°35′ N, 78°49′ E
T	Mound: 100 m^2, 6 m high
C	Late Historical P.
D	Sherds Beads Mud-bricks, burnt bricks
LF	
R	Singh 1979, 79
N	

29. Bedpur	
L	27°43′ N, 79°05′ E
T	Mound: 210 × 140 m, 8 m high

C	Late Historical P.
D	Sherds: RW Terracotta discs, wheels Brickbats
LF	
R	Singh 1979, 97
N	

30. Bhaduya Math or Bhaduivamath	
L	27°27′30″ N, 79°08′30″ E
T	Temple: 12 m^2
C	Late Historical P.
D	Hindu sculptures Remains of a limestone temple, in the *nagara* style
LF	Sculptures *in situ*
R	Singh 1979, 48-9 Singh 1984 ?, 8
N	

31. Bhadwas Sarai	
L	27°38′ N, 78°30′ E
T	Mound: 100 × 60 m, 9 m high Fort
C	Late Historical P.
D	• Mound: Sherds Few sculptures Brickbats

	• Fort: Mud rampart with four towers, a inner enclosure wall with similar towers
LF	
R	Singh 1979, 77 Singh 1984 ?, 7
N	

32. Bhagiratha Gupha	
L	27°52′ N, 78°45′ E, 3 km from Soron
T	Mound
C	Late Historical P.
D	Hindu sculptures Little finds (not described)
LF	
R	Singh 1979, 57-8 Singh 1984 ?, 11
N	Near the mound a medieval temple and an earthen cave called Bhagiratha Gupha

33. Bharatpur	
L	27°49′30″ N, 78°45′30″ E
T	
C	Late Historical P.
D LF	Colossal limestone statue of Hanuman
R	Singh 1979, 57
N	

34. Bhargain	
L	27°35′34″ N, 79°08′57″ E
T	Mound: 160 × 140 m, 6 m high Tombs
C	PGW cult., NBPW cult., Late Historical P., Sultanate, Mughal periods
D	• Mound: Sherds: PGW, GW, NBPW, BRW, BPW, RW, RSW Terracotta finds: animal and human figurines, discs, beads Remains of a fortress, brickbats • Tombs: Several tombs in *lakhauri* bricks
LF	
R	*IAR* 1959-60, 75 Singh 1979, 27 Shrimali 1983, vol. I, 196 Singh 1984 ?, 3 Ghosh 1989, vol. 2, 67 Chakrabarti et al. 2002, 115
N	Local tradition: ermitage site of the sage Bhrigu Terracotta discs similar to those found at Sravasti, Hastinapura P. III

35. Bhartauli	
L	27°29′ N, 78°41′ E
T C	Mound: 60 × 30 m, 2 m high Late Historical P.
D	Sherds Terracotta figurine Brickbats Remains of brick-foundation walls joined with mortar .

LF	
R	Singh 1979, 71
N	

36. Bhilauli	
L	27°49′ N, 78°49′30″ E
T	Fort: 30 m², 5 m high
C	Late Historical P., Sultanate, Mughal periods
D	Mud citadel (*garhi*) with four towers and moat
LF	
R	Singh 1979, 84
N	Traditionally erected by Nawab Bungas of Farrukhabad

37. Bhojpur	
L	27°37′ N, 78°54′ E
T	Mound: 2 acres, 3 m high
C	Late Historical P.
D	Sherds
LF	
R	Singh 1979, 92
N	

38. Bilauti	
L	27°38′30″ N, 78°54′ E
T	Mound: 110 × 75 m, 10 m high
C	Late Historical P.

D	Sherds: GW, BSW with painted designs Terracotta finds: animal figurine, bead, quern
LF	Numerous sculptures collected in a recent temple
R	Singh 1979, 93
N	

39. Bilram	
L	27°49′30″ N, 78°35′ E
T	Mound: 60 × 30 m, 1.5 m high Tombs Mosques Well *Sati* post
C	Late Historical P., Sultanate, Mughal periods
D	Numerous Hindu, Jaina, Buddhist sculptures (Gurjara-Pratihara) 6 fragmentary epitaphs (Thirteenth century AD) • Tombs: Tomb of Muhammad Makhdum Salahuddin Chisti and several graves in the same enclosure W of village few graves with epigraphs • Well constructed in bricks (51 × 25.5 × 12.51 cm)
LF	
R	*IAR* 1966-7, 61 Singh 1979, 55 Singh 1984 ?, 9
N	Local tradition: Site of Dhiraj Chauhan (?)

40. Bilsad or Bilsar or Bilsand or Bilsari	excavated
L	27°33′02″ N, 79°11′39″ E Mound 1, south of village Mound 2, west of village Mound 3, on the village
T	Mound 1: 230 × 150 m, 6 m high Mound 2: d. 50 m, 6 m high Mound 3: 50 × 40 m, 10 m high
C	PGW cult., NBPW cult., Kushan period, Late Historical P.
D	• Mound 1: Sherds: GW, NBPW, RW Terracotta animal figurines • Mound 2 (circular shape): Sherds: PGW, NBPW, RW • Mound 3: Sherds: GW, BW, RW Terracotta mutilated figurines Some sculptures (Gupta and later) 4 pillars: two bearing inscriptions of Kumaragupta (AD 415)
LF	
R	Singh 1979, 31 Shrimali 1983, vol. I, 196 Singh 1984 ?, 4-5 Ghosh 1989, vol. 2, 78 Chakrabarti et al. 2002, 115
N	Identified by Cunningham with Pi-lo-shan-na (of Hsuan Tsang), and also with Talsanda (of Muslim historians) Mound 1: ware similar to that found at Hastinapura P. IV Mound 2: maybe a *stupa*

41. Chhitauni	
L	27°45′ N, 78°54′ E
T	Mound: 30 × 30 m, 6 m high Fort: 40 m^2, 6 m high
C	Late Historical P., Sultanate, Mughal periods
D	Hindu sculptures • Mound: Sherds: RW occasionally decorated Terracotta finds: spindle whorls, broken female plaque 2 wells in bricks and limestone • Fort: Ruins of walls and bastions in mud bricks
LF	
R	Singh 1979, 91 Singh 1984 ?, 10
N	

42. Datauli	
L	27°28′ N, 78°51′ E
T	Mound: 130 × 80 m, 3 m high
C	Late Historical P.
D	Sherds Sculptures Brickbats
LF	
R	Singh 1979, 89
N	Traditionally it was a *garhi*

43. Daudganj	
L	27°28′ N, 79°10′ E
T	Temples (two)
C	Late Historical P., Sultanate, Mughal periods
D	Hindu sculptures Ruined temples in *lakhauri* bricks, with a single cella
LF	
R	Singh 1979, 100
N	

44. Daulesar	
L	
T	Fort
C	Late Historical P.
D	Remains of a fort of Chauhans
LF	
R	Singh 1979, 102
N	

45. Dhamri	
L	Fort, south-west of village
T	Fort
C	Late Historical P.
D	Remains of a mud fort
LF	
R	Singh 1979, 102
N	

46. Etah	
L	27°33′30″ N, 78°41′12″ E; *tahsil* Etah
T	
C	Late Historical P.
D	Several sculptures
LF	
R	*IAR* 1958-9, 74
N	

47. Firozpur Silauni	
L	27°46′ N, 78°35′ E Mound 1, north-west of village Mound 2, south-west of village
T	Mound 1: 5 acres, 3 m high Mound 2: 6 acres, 3 m high Well Tombs
C	Late Historical P.; Sultanate, Mughal periods
D	• Mounds (1 and 2): Sherds Brickbats • Well in *lakhauri* bricks, with Persian inscription • Tombs in *lakhauri* bricks
LF	
R	*IAR* 1959-60, 63 Singh 1979, 78 Singh 1984 ?, 11
N	

48. Garh	
L	27°20′ N, 78°17′ E
T	Mound: 300 × 200 m, 8 m high
C	PGW cult., NBPW cult., Kushan period, Late Historical P.
D	Sherds: GW, RSW, NBPW, BSW, bPW, RW (Kushan) Terracotta finds: beads, wheels, incense-burners Buddhist, Hindu sculptures (Gurjara-Pratihara)
LF	
R	Singh 1979, 31 Shrimali 1983, vol. I, 197 Singh 1984 ?, 5
N	

49. Garhi	
L	27°36′ N, 78°49′ E
T	Mound: 4 acres, 3 m high
C	Late Historical P.
D	Sherds Brickbats
LF	
R	Singh 1979, 80
N	

50. Garhi Kharai	
L	Mound 2, east of mound 1
T	Mound 1: 6 acres Mound 2: 100 m^2, 1 m high

C	Late Historical P.; Sultanate, Mughal periods
D	• Mound 1: Sherds: RW, GW Terracotta beads, balls Fort 40 m^2, in mud and burnt bricks, with towers and rampart • Mound 2: Platform (5 m^2) in *lakhauri* bricks
LF	
R	Singh 1979, 98
N	

51. Gehrana	
L	27°30′ N, 78°29′ E
T	Mound: 210 × 100 m, 12 m high
C	Late Historical P.
D	Sherds Terracotta beads Brickbats
LF	
R	Singh 1979, 69-70
N	Remains of a fortress (?)

52. Ghaitu	
L	27°31′30″ N, 78°29′ E
T	Mound: 100 × 50 m, 3 m high
C	Late Historical P.

D	Sherds Terracotta figurines Sculptures Brickbats
LF	
R	Singh 1979, 70
N	

53. Ghumaria

L	27°27′ N, 78°41′ E
T	Mound
C	Gurjara-Pratihara period
D	Hindu sculptures (Gurjara-Pratihara)
LF	Sculptures collected in a recent temple on the mound
R	Singh 1979, 76
N	

54. Gonar

L	27°45′30″ N, 78°51′ E Mound, 1 km south of village
T	Mound: 1 acre, 1 m high
C	Late Historical P.
D	Sherds: RW
LF	
R	Singh 1979, 90
N	

55. Gothua	
L	27°23′ N, 78°18′ E
T	Mound: 60 m^2, 3 m high
C	Late Historical P.
D	Sherds Hindu sculptures Structural fragments
LF	
R	Singh 1979, 100
N	

56. Gurahna	
L	27°52′ N, 78°40′ E
T	Mound: 160 × 100 m, 2 m high
C	Late Historical P.
D	Sherds: RW Terracotta beads
LF	
R	Singh 1979, 87
N	

57. Harnather	
L	27°52′30″ N, 78°35′ E Mound, north of village
T	Mound: 100 × 30 m, 1 m high
C	Late Historical P.

D	Sherds: RW Buddhist, Hindu medieval sculptures Brickbats Foundation walls
LF	
R	Singh 1979, 67-8
N	

58. Harnathpur	
L	27°53′30″ N, 78°37′ E Mound, 2 km north-east of village
T	Mound: 200 m^2, 2 m high
C	Late Historical P.
D	Sherds Brickbats
LF	
R	Singh 1979, 88
N	

59. Himmatnagar Bajhera	
L	
T	Mound
C	Late Historical P.
D	Finds not described
LF	
R	Singh 1984 ?, 7
N	

60. Intwa	
L	27°51′ N, 78°33′30″ E
T	
C	Late historical P.
D	Buddhist sculptures (tenth-eleventh century AD)
LF	
R	Singh 1979, 54
N	

61. Isara Panchhayan Pati or Ishara	
L	27°23′ N, 78°49′30″ E
T	Mound: 160 × 60 m, 10 m high Temple
C	Late Historical P.
D	• Mound: Sherds: BW, RW Brickbats (51 × 25.5 × 9 cm, 40.5 × 25.5 × 7.5 cm) Foundation walls • Temple (ruined): Terracotta heads Friezes Pillars Limestone plint (25 × 16 m, 2 m high)
LF	
R	Singh 1979, 87 Singh 1984 ?, 8
N	

62. Jahangirabad	
L	27°25′ N, 78°47′ E
T	Mound: 50 × 15 m, 2 m high
C	Late Historical P.
D	Sherds Terracottas Bricks (35.5 × 20.5 × 6.5 cm)
LF	
R	Singh 1979, 74
N	

63. Jakhera	excavated
L	27°48′02″ N, 78°35′22″ E Mound, 8 km west of Kasganj
T	Mound: 380 × 210 m, 13 m high
C	PGW cult., NBPW cult.
D	Sherds: BRW, PGW, NBPW, BPW, GW, BSW, RW, bSW, perforated ware Terracotta finds: human and animal figurines, discs, balls, pendants, beads, spindle whorls, gamesmen, geometrical objects Stone pestle, balls Beads in various materials Bone objects: arrow-heads and points Copper objects: bangle and 'antimony rod', hooks, needle Iron objects: axes, sickle, arrow heads, cesels, nails and slags Nodules and slices of quartz and jasper Remains of structural activity: floors, post-holes Low mud embankment (4.80 m, 80 cm high) Canals

LF	
R	*IAR* 1959-60, 75 *IAR* 1974-5, 43-5 *IAR* 1975-6, 50-1 *IAR* 1986-7, 77-8 Singh 1979, 26-7 Shrimali 1983, vol. I, 198 Roy 1983, 27-8 Singh 1984 ?, 2 Possehl 1986, 45 Ghosh 1989, vol. 2, 180 Chakrabarti et al. 2002, 116
N	Terracotta discs similar to those found in Hastinapur P. III Traditionally founded by Raja Bali; ancient name: Yajña-Khera or Yaksha-Khera Local name: Kusak

64. Jakhirudrapur	
L	27°50′ N, 78°39′ E
T	Mound: 50 × 30 m, 2 m high
C	Late Historical P.
D	Sherds
LF	
R	Singh 1979, 82
N	

65. Jalesar or Jalesar Fort	
L	27°28′16″ N, 78°18′23″ E; *tahsil* Jalesar H.Q.
T	Mound: circumf. 1 km, 22 m high Tombs

C	PGW cult., NBPW cult., Sunga-Kushan period, Late Historical P., sixteenth-eighteenth century AD
D	• Mound: Sherds: GW, NBPW, RW, RPW, glazed ware, others (?) Terracotta finds: human and animal figurines, beads Glass beads Copper and iron objects Limestone Hindu sculptures • Tombs: Few tombs with Persian inscriptions (sixteenth-eighteenth century AD)
LF	
R	*IAR* 1966-7, 33 *IAR* 1975-6, 70 *IAR* 1986-7, 115 Singh, 1979, 30 Shrimali 1983, vol. I, 198 Singh 1984 ?, 5 Ghosh 1989, vol. 2, 181 Chakrabarti et al. 2002, 116
N	

66. Jamun	
L	27°28′ N, 78°15′ E
T	Mound: 60 m^2, 3 m high
C	Late Historical P.
D	Sherds Terracotta head Few Jaina sculptures Brickbats

LF	
R	Singh 1979, 102
N	

67. Janak Khera	
L	27°39′30″ N, 78°55′30″ E
T	Mound: 200 × 100 m, 3 m high
C	Late Historical P.
D	Sherds: RW, GW, BSW Terracotta animal figurines Brickbats
LF	
R	Singh 1979, 92
N	

68. Jauhari	
L	27°47′ N, 78°51′30″ E
T	Mound: 200 × 130 m, 10 m high
C	Tenth-eleventh century AD
D	Sherds: RW Stone pestle Hindu sculptures
LF	
R	Singh 1979, 93
N	

69. Jhinwar	
L	27°31′30″ N, 78°30′30″ E Mound 1, W of village Mound 2, NE of village Mound 3, E of village
T	Mound 1: 150 × 50 m, 6 m high Mound 2: 60 × 30 m, 2 m high Mound 3: 50 × 30 m, 1.8 m high
C	Late Historical P.
D	• Mound 1: Sherds Terracottas Brickbats • Mound 2: Remains of a fortress (?) • Mound 3: Sherds Terracottas
LF	
R	Singh 1979, 70
N	

70. Kabar	
L	27°28′ N, 78°44′ E
T	Mound: 100 × 30 m, 13 m high
C	Late Historical P.
D	Sherds Brickbats

LF	
R	Singh 1979, 73
N	

71. Kadirbari or Kadarbari	
L	27°55′30″ N, 78°45′ E
T	Fort
C	Late Historical P.
D	Sherds: RW, BSW Terracotta caprisoned-horse Iron lamp *Garhi* with two enclosure walls (90 × 75 m, 10 × 10 m) and remains of towers
LF	
R	Singh 1979, 85-6 Singh 1984 ?, 7
N	

72. Kadirganj	
L	
T	Mound
C	Late Historical P.
D	Finds not described
LF	
R	Singh 1979, 102
N	

73. Kakrala	
L	27°36′30″ N, 79°05′ E Mound, 1 km north-west of village
T	Mound: 135 m^2, 5 m high
C	Late Historical P.
D	Sherds Foundation walls Well in bricks (30.5 × 10 × 7.5 cm)
LF	
R	Singh 1979, 97
N	

74. Kalinjar	
L	27°27′ N, 79°13′ E
T	Mound: 130 × 60 m, 3 m high
C	Kushan period, Gupta period, Gurjara-Pratihara period
D	Sherds: RW (Kushan) *c.* 190 terracotta human figurines (Kushan, Gupta and later) Hindu sculptures (Gurjara-Pratihara)
LF	
R	Singh 1979, 45-7
N	The site was probably a warehouse of terracottas

75. Kalyanpur	
L	27°49′ N, 78°45′30″ E
T	Mound: 130 × 100 m, 3 m high
C	Late Historical P.

D	Sherds: GW
LF	
R	Singh 1979, 83
N	Several decorated (painted) sherds

76. Kamsan	
L	
T	Mound
C	NBPW cult., Late Historical P.
D	Sherds: NBPW Sculptures
LF	
R	Singh 1984 ?, 6
N	

77. Kartala	
L	27°34′ N, 78°49′30″ E
T	Mound: 1 acre, 6 m high
C	Late Historical P.
D	Finds not described
LF	
R	Singh 1979, 80
N	

78. Karthani	
L	27°25′ N, 78°19′ E
T	Mound: 5 acres, 1 m high
C	Late Historical P.
D	Sherds Brickbats
LF	
R	Singh 1979, 99
N	

79. Kasaulia	
L	27°31′ N, 79°01′ E, *tahsil* Aliganj
T	Temple
C	*c.* Eighth-Ninth century
D	*Kankar* slabs Architectural carved members Structural remains
LF	
R	*IAR* 1995-6, 88
N	Site traditionally called as *devasthana* Near the site existed an extensive mound, now levelled

80. Kawar	
L	27°28′17″ N, 78°43′44″ E
T	Mound: *c.* 10 ha, *c.* 10 m high
C	Early century AD
D	Sherds

LF	
R	Chakrabarti et al. 2002, 116
N	

81. Khera	
L	27°28′ N, 78°32′ E Mound E of village
T	Mound Temples
C	Late Historical P.
D	• Mound: Sherds Brickbats • Temples (plinths): Hindu, Jaina sculptures (ninth-tenth century AD) Inscription on the pedestal of a panel Brickbats (33 × 18 × 5 cm, 25.5 × 25.5 × 10 cm) 2 plinths in limestone
LF	
R	Singh 1979, 80 Singh 1984 ?, 8
N	

82. Khiria Banar	
L	27°31′ N, 79°02′30″ E
T	Mound: 60 m^2, 3 m high
C	Late Historical P.
D	Sherds: RW Terracotta ball

LF	
R	Singh 1979, 97
N	

83. Kilarmau	
L	
T	Mound
C	Late Historical P.
D	Hindu, Buddhist sculptures
LF	
R	Singh 1984?, 10
N	

84. Kilauni Rifatpur	
L	27°51′ N, 78°39′ E
T	Mound: 130 × 100 m, 5 m high
C	Late Historical P.
D	Sherds
LF	
R	Singh 1979, 86
N	

85. Kindi	
L	27°56′30″ N, 78°36′ E
T	Mound: 2 acres, 1 m high
C	Late Historical P.

D	Sherds: RW, GW Brickbats
LF	
R	Singh 1979, 88
N	

86. Kisrauli	
L	27°53′ N, 78°36′ E
T	Temple: 5 × 5 m
C	Late Historical P., Sultanate, Mughal periods
D	Hindu sculptures Temple in *lakhaurī* bricks
LF	
R	Singh 1979, 56-7
N	

87. Kucharhani	
L	27°39′ N, 78°54′ E
T	Mound: 160 × 100 m, 1 m high
C	Late Historical P.
D	Sherds: RW Brickbats (55 × 25.5 × 7.5 cm) Foundation walls in limestone and bricks Well in limestone and bricks
LF	
R	Singh 1979, 91
N	

88. Kudesa	
L	27°28′19″ N, 79°11′30″ E
T	Mound: 300 × 200 m, 16 m high Temple: 10 m^2
C	Late Historical P.
D	Sculptures, floral friezes • Mound: Sherds Copper coin Large wedge-shaped bricks *Kankar* scraps, tiles, structural fragments • Temple: Foundation walls in limestone
LF	Architectural members and sculptures collected in a recent temple, north of site
R	Singh 1979, 98-9 Singh 1984 ?, 7
N	

89. Kupoli	
L	27°46′ N, 79°06′ E
T	Mound: 100 m^2, 6 m high
C	Late Historical P.
D	Sherds Terracotta beads
LF	
R	Singh 1979, 94
N	

90. Kusura	
L	27°28′30″ N, 78°24′30″ E
T	Mound: 60 m^2, 4 m high
C	Late Historical P.
D	Sherds
LF	
R	Singh 1979, 99
N	

91. Laher	
L	27°53′ N, 78°41′ E Mound 2, south of Mound 1
T	Mound 2: 100 × 60 m, 2 m high
C	Late Historical P.
D	• Mound 1: Remains of a *garhi*, with vestiges of towers, erected in mud (50 × 40 m, 6 m high) • Mound 2: Sherds: RW, BSW, others (?)
LF	
R	Singh 1979, 87
N	*Garhi* beside the course of the old Ganga

92. Lohari Khera	
L	27°33′41″ N, 79°04′42 E
T	Mound: 60 m^2, 2 m high
C	Late Historical P.

D	Sherds: RW
LF	
R	Singh 1979, 97
N	

93. Lohiakhera	
L	
T	
C	Sunga-Kushan period, Late Historical P.
D	Sherds: GW, BSW, RW, others (?)
LF	
R	*IAR* 1970-1, 37 Shrimali 1983, vol. I, 199 Ghosh 1989, vol. 2, 257
N	

94. Loya Khar	
L	27°31′ N, 78°51′ E
T	Temple (ruins)
C	Late Historical P.
D	Terracottas Hindu, Buddhist sculptures Stone tiles, slabs Foundation wall in bricks (45.5 × 23 × 7.5 cm)
LF	
R	Singh 1979, 79 Singh 1984 ?, 9
N	

95. Mahewa Khera	
L	27°27′30″ N, 78°52′30″ E
T	Mound: 16 m^2, 6 m high
C	Late Historical P.
D	Sherds Terracottas Remains of four towers; moat
LF	
R	Singh 1979, 89
N	*Garhi* of Rahmat-ullah (?)

96. Majhrau	
L	27°30′05″ N, 78°32′ E
T	Mound: 60 × 50 m, 9 m high Temple: 10 m^2
C	Late Historical P.
D	• Mound: Sherds Brickbats • Temple: Sculptures Limestone plinth Structural remains
LF	
R	Singh 1979, 69
N	

97. Malagaon	
L	
T	Mound
C	Late Historical P.
D	Hindu sculptures
LF	
R	Singh 1984 ?, 10
N	

98. Malgawan	
L	27°24′ N, 78°46′ E
T	Mound: 140 × 90 m, 10 m high
C	Late Historical P.
D	Sherds: BPW, BRW, RW, GW Hindu sculptures Brickbats (30.5 × 20.5 × 5 cm)
LF	
R	Singh 1979, 73-4
N	*Garhi* of Chauhan chieftains

99. Margayan or Maragayan	
L	27°34′ N, 78°28′ E
T	Mound: 140 × 45 m, 6 m high Tank
C	Late Historical P.

D	• Mound: Sherds Terracotta figurines Hindu sculptures Brickbats Pillars, pilasters, jamb • Tank: Stepped, erected in bricks
LF	
R	Singh 1979, 66 Singh 1984 ?, 9
N	

100. Medupur	
L	27°35′16″ N, 79°08′ E Mound east of village
T	Mound: 1 acre, 2 m high Well
C	Late Historical P.
D	• Mound: Sherds • Well in bricks (25.5 × 16.5 × 6.5 cm)
LF	
R	Singh 1979, 99
N	

101. Mehuta	
L	27°27′24″ N, 79°11′10″ E Mound 1, north of village Mound 2, the village

T	Mound 1: 60 m^2, 2 m high Mound 2: 0.5 acre, 3 m high
C	Late Historical P.
D	• Mound 1 and 2: Sherds Brickbats
LF	
R	Singh 1979, 99
N	

102. Mira Kalan	
L	27°29′ N, 78°26′ E
T	Mound: 100 × 80 m, 6.5 m high
C	Late Historical P.
D	Sherds
LF	
R	Singh 1979, 99
N	

103. Mohi-ud-Dinpur	
L	27°40′05″ N, 78°32′ E
T	Mound: 200 × 60 m, 2 m high
C	Late Historical P.
D	Sherds Brickbats Hindu sculptures
LF	A sculpture installed in a recent temple

R	Singh 1979, 77 Singh 1984 ?, 9
N	

104. Mohi-ud-Dipur or Mohiddipur	
L	27°37′ N, 78°52′ E
T	Mound: 40 m^2, 2 m high
C	Late Historical P.
D LF	Sherds Hindu sculptures Carved slabs Stone tiles, beams
R	Singh 1979, 78
N	Presence of an old (?) temple

105. Muhammadpur	
L	27°52′30″ N, 78°51′ E
T	Mound: 25 m^2, 3 m high
C	Late Historical P.
D	Sherds
LF	
R	Singh 1979, 89
N	

106. Nadara	
L	
T	Mound
C	Late Historical P.
D	Finds not described
LF	
R	Singh 1984 ?, 9
N	

107. Nadir	
L	27°36′ N, 78°28′ E
T	Mound: 160 × 100 m, 8 m high
C	Late Historical P.
D	Sherds Beads Hindu sculptures Brickbats
LF	Sculptures spotted over limestone platform
R	Singh 1979, 73
N	

108. Nadrai	
L	27°47′ N, 78°37′ E Mound 1, west of temple Mound 2, east of village
T	Mound 1: 50 m^2, 10 m high Mound 2: d. 13 m, 5 m high Temple

C	Late Historical P.; Sultanate, Mughal periods
D	Medieval sculptures • Mound 1: Sherds: GW, BSW, bSW Remains of four towers and thee gateways in *lakhauri* bricks • Mound 2: Sherds Brickbats Hindu sculptures Foundation walls of different structures • Temple in *lakhauri* bricks
LF	
R	Singh 1979, 60 Singh 1984 ?, 11
N	

109. Nagla Ajit	
L	27°38′ N, 78°59′ E
T	Mound: 160 × 130 m, 3 m high
C	Late Historical P.
D	Sherds: RW Carved jamb Brickbats
LF	
R	Singh 1979, 95
N	

110. Nagla Bhikhari	
L	27°35′ N, 78°54′ E
T	Mound: 100 m², 1 m high
C	Late Historical P.
D	Sherds: RW Brickbats
LF	
R	Singh 1979, 93
N	

111. Nagla Damar	
L	27°47′ N, 79°02′ E
T	Mound: 100 × 60 m, 6 m high
C	Late Historical P.
D	Sherds: RW
LF	
R	Singh 1979, 95
N	

112. Nagla Dhimar	
L	27°29′30″ N, 78°53′ E
T	Mound: 16 m², 2 m high
C	Late Historical P.
D	Sherds Brickbats (25.5 × 20.5 × 5 cm)

LF	
R	Singh 1979, 89
N	Traditionally there was a palace of a certain Rathor

113. Nagla Duria	
L	27°34′ N, 78°51′ E
T	Mound: 1 acre, 3 m high
C	Late Historical P.
D	Sherds Terracottas Sculptures Brickbats
LF	
R	Singh 1979, 80
N	

114. Nagla Garhi Lalpur	
L	27°26′ N, 78°58′ E
T	Mound: 80 × 50 m, 5 m high
C	Late Historical P.
D	Sherds Brickbats
LF	
R	Singh 1979, 99
N	

115. Nagla Kothi	
L	27°43′30″ N, 78°52′ E
T	Fort: 150 × 95 m Temple
C	Late Historical P.
D	• Fort erected in mud and burnt bricks, with rampart and ditch: Sherds: GW, bSW, RW Terracotta gamesman, wheels, beads, balls Roughly dressed stone object • Temple in limestone
LF	
R	Singh 1979, 94
N	

116. Namaini	
L	27°55′ N, 78°36′ E
T	Mound: 1 acre, 3 m high
C	Late Historical P.
D	Sherds: RW Brickbats
LF	
R	Singh 1979, 85
N	

117. Narahara	
L	27°34′ N, 78°42′ E
T	Mound: 1 acre, 3 m high

C	Late Historical P.
D	Sherds Brickbats
LF	
R	Singh 1979, 74
N	

118. Naurauli	
L	27°31′ N, 78°23′ E
T	
C	Gurjara-Pratihara period
D	Hindu sculptures
LF	
R	Singh 1979, 44-5 Singh 1984 ?, 9
N	

119. Narauli	
L	27°52′ N, 78°37′30″ E
T	Mound
C	Late Historical P.
D	Sherds: RW Limestone Hindu sculptures Brickbats
LF	
R	Singh 1979, 85
N	

120. Nardauli	
L	27°45′ N, 79°07′ E
T	Mound: 3 acres, 5 m high
C	Late Historical P.
D	Sherds: RW, GW Brickbats
LF	
R	Singh 1979, 95
N	

121. Naurtha	
L	27°52′30″ N, 78°39′30″ E
T	Mound: 1 acre, 2 m high
C	Late Historical P.
D	Sherds Terracotta beads
LF	
R	Singh 1979, 86
N	

122. Nausana	
L	27°44′ N, 79°06′ E
T	Mound: 100 × 60 m, 6 m high
C	Late Historical P.
D	Sherds: RW
LF	

R	Singh 1979, 96
N	

123. Nawabganj	
L	27°49′ N, 78°46′ E
T	Mound: 110 × 75 m, 6 m high
C	Late Historical P.
D	Sherds: GW, BPW Terracotta animal figurine Ruins of an enclosure wall and towers Well in bricks
LF	
R	Singh 1979, 83 Singh 1984 ?, 7
N	

124. Nidhauli	
L	
T	Fort
C	Late Historical P.
D	Remains not described
LF	
R	Singh 1979, 103
N	Fort erected by Khusal Singh

125. Nokhas	
L	
T	Mound
C	Late Historical P.
D	Sculptures
LF	
R	*IAR* 1957-8, 69
N	Among the sculptures the famous Rukhini image

126. Nokhera	
L	27°35′ N, 78°25′ E
T	Mound: 8 acres, 9 m high
C	PGW cult., NBPW cult., Late Historical P.
D	Sherds: PGW, GW, BRW, RW, NBPW, BPW, BSW Hindu sculptures (Gurjara-Pratihara)
LF	
R	*IAR* 1957-8, 69 *IAR* 1960-1, 66 Tripathi 1976, 129 Singh 1979, 29 Shrimali 1983, vol. I, 200 Singh 1984 ?, 2 Roy 1986, xvii Ghosh 1989, vol. 2, 319
N	Traditionally associated with Bhishma and with a fort erected by him

127. Pachgain Khas	
L	27°52′30″ N, 78°34′30″ E
T	Mound: 100 × 61 m, 2 m high
C	Late Historical P.
D	Sherds: RW Brickbats
LF	
R	Singh 1979, 88
N	

128. Patiali	
L	27°41′35″ N, 78°59′59″ E Mound 2, east of town Mosque, south of town
T	Mound 1: circumf. 930 m, 22 m high Mound 2: 62 m^2, 3 m high Fort Tombs Wells Mosque Temple
C	Sunga period, Kushan period, Late Historical P.; Sultanate, Mughal periods
D	Numerous sculptures, in sandstone and limestone (Gurjara-Pratihara) Fragmentary inscriptions of Alauddin Khalji and Akbar • Mound 1: Sherds Hindu sculptures Brickbats

	• Mound 2: Sherds (Kushan) • Fort in ruins with rampart in limestone (10 m high) • 3 tombs in *lakhauri* bricks • Mosque • Wells in bricks and limestone, with Persian and Arabic inscriptions
LF	Sculptures scattered in the village
R	*IAR* 1966-7, 61 Singh 1979, 50-3 Singh 1984 ?, 6 Chakrabarti et al. 2002, 115
N	Traditionally the site is connected with King Drupad Mound 2 known as Drona Tila Site referred in the *Tarikh-i-Firozshah* by Jia-ul-Barni There had been 35 temples (?)

129. Phapotu	
L	27°27′ N, 78°40′ E
T	Temple Mound: 160 × 100 m, 20 m high
C	Late Historical P.
D	• Temple (ruined): Hindu sculptures (Gurjara-Pratihara) Carved stones Foundation structure (13 × 6 m) • Mound: Sherds Brickbats
LF	

R	Singh 1979, 72 Singh 1984 ?, 8
N	

130. Pilkhuni	
L	27°40′ N, 78°51′ E
T	Fort: 80 m^2
C	Late Historical P., Sultanate period
D	Sherds: RW Rampart in mud bricks with four bastions (16 m high) in burnt bricks and a ditch (5 m width)
LF	
R	Singh 1979, 92-3 Singh 1984 ?, 7
N	

131. Pilwa	
L	27°37′ N, 78°34′ E
T	Temple Mosque Well
C	Late Historical P.; Sultanate, Mughal periods
D	• Temple (repaired): Foundation walls and plinth in limestone • Mosque in limestone, plastered • Well in limestone
LF	
R	Singh 1979, 74-5
N	

132. Pinjari	
L	27°26′30″ N, 79°02′20″ E; *tahsil* Aliganj
T	Temple
C	*c.* Eighth-ninth century
D	Temple (in ruins) in *kankar*-slabs
LF	
R	*IAR* 1995-6, 88-9
N	

133. Pipahra	
L	27°29′30″ N, 78°45′30″ E Mound, 800 m south of village
T	Mound: 40 × 15 m, 1 m high
C	Late Historical P.
D	Sherds Bricks (30.5 × 21.5 × 6.5 cm)
LF	
R	Singh 1979, 74
N	

134. Pipargaon	
L	27°27′30″ N, 79°13′20″ E
T	Mound: 180 × 100 m, 8 m high
C	PGW cult., NBPW cult.
D	Sherds: PGW, GW, NBPW, BPW, BSW, bSW, BRW, RW
LF	

R	*IAR* 1959-60, 75 Singh 1979, 28 Shrimali 1983, vol. I, 200 Singh 1984 ?, 3 Roy 1986, xvii Ghosh 1989, vol. 2, 345
N	Identified with Pippalagrama, near Kampilya, referred in the *Brihatkathakosa* (Singh 1979)

135. Piwari	
L	
T	Mound
C	Late Historical P.
D	Sherds Brickbats Carved door-jamb
LF	
R	Singh 1979, 103
N	

136. Pondri	
L	27°28′ N, 78°24′30″ E
T	Tower
C	Late Historical P.
D	Hindu sculptures (Gurjara-Pratihara) Remains of a tower originally in mud bricks, renovated in burnt bricks
LF	

R	Singh 1979, 45
N	The site was an old (?) fortress

137. Puranpur	
L	27°51′30″ N, 78°50′12″ E
T	Mound 1: 40 × 30 m, 3 m high Mound 2: 1 acre, 1 m high
C	Late Historical P.
D	Sherds
LF	
R	Singh 1979, 90
N	Mound 1: called *garhi* without any trace of thc citadel

138. Puraon	
L	27°29′ N, 78°47′ E
T	Mound: 80 × 30 m, 5 m high
C	Late Historical P.
D	Sherds Terracotta figurines Brickbats Remains of foundation walls
LF	
R	Singh 1979, 71
N	

139. Pursari	
L	27°37′ N, 78°59′ E Mound 1, west of village Mound 2, north-west of village
T	Mound 1: 1 acre, 3 m high Mound 2: 4 acres, 2 m high Temple
C	Late Historical P.
D	• Mound 1: Sherds Brickbats • Mound 2: Regional pottery Other finds (not described) • Temple: Hindu sculptures Architectural fragments Limestone plinth and square terrace (10 m)
LF	Several sculptures collected in a recent temple
R	Singh 1979, 53-4
N	

140. Raipur Mothra	
L	27°38′36″ N, 79°01′30″ E
T	Mound: 4 acres, 3 m high
C	Late Historical P.
D	RW, BPW Brickbats Remains of foundation walls

LF	
R	Singh 1979, 95
N	

141. Rijaur	
L	
T	Mound
C	Ninth -Tenth century AD
D	Hindu, Jaina sculptures
LF	
R	Singh 1984 ?, 9
N	

142. Rijor Khas	
L	27°24′26″ N, 78°42′29″ E Mound 1, north of village Mound 3, south of village Mound 4, north-east of village Mound 5, at a distance of 500 m
T	Mound 1: 60 × 30 m, 6 m high Mound 2: 600 × 400 m, 20 m high Mound 3: 16 m^2, 2 m high Mound 4: d. 30 m, 10 m high Mound 5: 13 × 6 m, 2 m high
C	NBPW cult., Late Historical P.
D	Sculptures (Gurjara-Pratihara) Microlithic point in crystal quartz • Mound 1: Sherds

	Brickbats Hindu sculptures Carved limestone fragments • Mound 2: Sherds Brickbats Coins Remains of mud structures • Mound 3: Sherds Brickbats • Mound 4: Sherds Brickbats Rectangular limestone plinth • Mound 5: Sherds Brickbats
LF	
R	Singh 1979, 63-6 Chakrabarti et al. 2002, 116
N	Traditionally is the ancient Rajat Kranti, of the *Mahabharata*.

143. Sadhera	
L	27°28′ N, 78°09′ E
T	Mound: 130 × 100 m, 3 m high
C	Late Historical P.
D	Sherds: RW, GW Brickbats Hindu sculpture

LF	
R	Singh 1979, 69
N	

144. Sahori	
L	*Tahsil* Patiali
T	Temple
C	Pratihara period
D	*Kankar* carved panels Structural and architectural members
LF	
R	*IAR* 1992-3, 116
N	

145. Sailai	
L	27°37′ N, 78°52′ E
T	Mound: 1 acre, 2 m high
C	Late Historical P.
D	Sherds: RW
LF	
R	Singh 1979, 92
N	

146. Sailot	
L	27°35′30″ N, 78°51′30″ E Tower, 500 m north of mound

T	Mound: 100 m^2, 6 m high Tower
C	Late Historical P., Sultanate period
D	• Mound: Copper coin with Persian inscription Sherds Brickbats *Kaṇkar* fragments • Tower erected in bricks (30.5 × 20.5 × 10 cm)
LF	
R	Singh 1979, 79 Singh 1984 ?, 7
N	

147. Saintra	
L	27°33′ N, 78°30′ E
T	Mound: 200 × 100 m, 12 m high
C	Late Historical P.
D	Sherds Terracotta fragments Sculptures Brickbats Foundation walls in burnt bricks, plastered
LF	
R	Singh 1979, 70
N	

148. Sakita or Sakit	
L	27°28′05″ N, 78°46′31″ E
T	Mound: 300 × 120 m, 20 m high Temple
C	PGW cult., Late Historical P.; Sultanate, Mughal periods
D	• Mound: Sherds: GW, BRW, RW, BPW Terracotta fragments Brickbats Well in *lakhauri* bricks • Temple unfinished, octagonal shape
LF	
R	*IAR* 1959-60, 63 *IAR* 1980-1, 71 Singh 1979, 61-2 Singh 1984 ?, 10-11 Chakrabarti et al. 2002, 116
N	Fort of Raja Sakit Singh or Sakit Das (?)

149. Salempur Piraunda	
L	27°47′ N, 78°31′ E
T	Mound: 70 × 40 m, 5 m high Fort
C	Late Historical P.
D	• Mound: Sherds: RW, others (?) • Fort (medieval) in mud and burnt bricks with a gateway and four corner towers

LF	
R	Singh 1979, 68
N	

150. Sarai Aghat	
L	27°21′ N, 79°16′ E
T	Mound: 260 × 200 m, 13 m high
C	Pre-Gupta period, Late Historical P.
D	Sherds: GW, BPW, BW, BSW, bPW, RPW Sculptures Terracotta plaque (pre-Gupta ?) Burnt bricks (38 × 23 × 7.5 cm, 42 × 24 × 7.5 cm)
LF	
R	Singh 1979, 101
N	Aghat or Agahet connected with the saint Agastya (?)

151. Sarawal	
L	27°35′ N, 78°54′30″ E Mound 1, on the village Mound 2, E of village
T	Mound 1: 80 × 60 m, 13 m high Mound 2: 210 × 160 m, 1 m high
C	Late Historical P.
D	• Mound 1: Sherds Brickbats Foundation walls and tower in mud and burnt bricks • Mound 2: Sherds: RW, GW Terracotta wheels

LF	
R	Singh 1979, 89-90 Singh 1984 ?, 7
N	Mound 2, locally called Nagaria, connected with a *garhi* (?)

152. Saunsah	
L	27°32′30″ N, 78°53′30″ E
T	Mound: 1 acre, 3 m high
C	Late Historical P.
D	Sherds Colossal Hindu medieval statue Brickbats
LF	Statue located in a recent temple
R	Singh 1979, 79
N	

153. Sena	
L	27°21′ N, 78°45′ E Mound 2, south of village Mound 3, north of village
T	Mound 1: 130 × 90 m, 20 m high Mound 2: 45 × 30 m, 3 m high Mound 3: d. 30 m, 9 m high
C	Late Historical P.
D	*Kankar* fragments • Mound 1: Sherds Bricks (35.5 × 25.5 × 9 cm, 38 × 28 × 9 cm, 32 × 25.5 × 9 cm)

	• Mound 2: Sherds • Mound 3: Sherds Sculptures
LF	
R	Singh 1979, 71-2 Singh 1984 ?, 7
N	Mound 1 connected with a fort erected by the king, Raja Parikshit (?) Mound 3 connected with the hermitage of *rshi* Bhringi (?)

154. Sewar	
L	27°51′ N, 78°35′30″ E
T	
C	Late Historical P.
D	Numerous terracottas Several Hindu sculptures
LF	
R	Singh 1979, 103
N	

155. Shahnagar Timarua	
L	27°26′ N, 78°15′ E
T	Mound: 115 × 65 m, 8 m high
C	PGW cult., Late Historical P.
D	Sherds: PGW, GW, BPW, bSW, RSW, RW Carved structural members Moat around the mound

LF	
R	Singh 1979, 27-8
N	

156. Shahpur	
L	
T	
C	PGW cult.
D	Sherds
LF	
R	*IAR* 1960-1, 66 Tripathi 1976, 130 Shrimali 1983, vol. I, 201
N	

157. Shyamsar	
L	27°53′ N, 78°46′ E Temple over the mound
T	Mound: 40 × 35 m, 6 m high Temple: 6.5 × 4.5 m, 5 m high
C	Late Historical P.; Sultanate, Mughal periods
D	• Mound: Sherds • Temple in limestone, restored in *lakhauri* bricks
LF	
R	Singh 1979, 54 Singh 1984 ?, 8
N	Temple built by the Nandadas (?)

158. Siddhpur	
L	27°38′ N, 78°52′ E
T	Mound: 3 acres, 3 m high
C	Late Historical P. to Thirteenth century AD
D	Sherds Hindu sculptures (twelfth-thirteenth century AD) Brickbats
LF	
R	Singh 1979, 54
N	

159. Sikaira	
L	27°41′ N, 78°54′30″ E Mound 2, 1 km south-east of village
T	Mound 1: 50 × 40 m, 6 m high Mound 2: 100 × 60 m, 1 m high
C	Late Historical P.
D	*Kankar* fragments • Mound 1: Sherds Brickbats Remains of mud towers at cardinal points Limestone well • Mound 2: Sherds
LF	
R	Singh 1979, 91-2 Singh 1984 ?, 7
N	

160. Sikandarpur	
L	27°37′27″ N, 79°07′28″ E
T	Mound: 3 acres, 3 m high
C	Late Historical P.
D	Sherds: RW, BSW Terracottas finds: balls, female head, sprinkler in Roman style (?)
LF	
R	Singh 1979, 98
N	

161. Sikandarpur Bais	
L	27°46′ N, 79°03′ E
T	Mound: 210 × 200 m, 12 m high
C	Late Historical P.
D	Sherds: RW, GW Mud bricks
LF	
R	Singh 1979, 96
N	Traditionally connected with the *garhi* of Raja Nidhi Singh

162. Sirsa Tippu	
L	27°40′17″ N, 78°38′13″ E
T	Mound: *c.* 2 ha, *c.* 1.5 m high
C	PGW cult.
D	Sherds: PGW, BRW, BSW

LF	
R	Chakrabarti et al. 2002, 116
N	

163. Sona	
L	27°26′ N, 78°19′ E
T	Mound: 220 × 120 m, 12 m high
C	PGW cult., NBPW cult., Late Historical P.
D	Sherds: PGW, GW, BSW, BRW, RW, bPW, NBPW, BPW Terracotta wheels, discs with notches
LF	
R	Singh 1979, 30 Shrimali 1983, vol. I, 202 Singh 1984 ?, 3
N	

164. Sonhar	
L	27°30′30″ N, 78°52′ E
T	Mound: 100 m^2, 12 m high
C	Late Historical P.
D	Sherds Bricks (30.5 × 20.5 × 6.5 cm)
LF	
R	Singh 1979, 90
N	Traditionally connected with Dhir Shah Rathor

165. Soron	
L	27°54′ N, 78°45′ E Mound 1, S of town
T	Mound 1: d. 10 m, 6 m high Mound 2: 400 m^2, 14 m high Temples (two) Tank: 14 m^2
C	Gupta period, Late Historical P. to Sixteenth century AD
D	Hindù sculptures (Gupta, Gurjara-Pratihara) Terracotta figurines (Gupta) Rectangular sandstone inscribed well tablet (AD 1324) • Mound 1: Sherds Limestone fragments, brickbats • Mound 2: Sherds: RW, BRW brickbats • Temple 1: Sita-Rama ji temple (twelfth century AD) with 75 pilgrim's epigraphs • Temple 2: Varaha temple in *lakhauri* bricks • Tank Surya Kunda
FL	
BR	*IAR* 1981-2, 87 Singh 1979, 58-60 Singh 1984 ?, 7
N	Sita-Rama ji temple located over Mound 2

166. Sujanpur	
L	27°46′ N, 78°44′ E
T	Mound: 60 × 16 m, 2 m high
C	Late Historical P.
D	Sherds Brickbats
LF	
R	Singh 1979, 81
N	

167. Suratpur	
L	27°47′ N, 78°41′30″ E
T	Mound: 115 × 100 m, 6 m high
C	Late Historical P.
D	Sherds Foundation walls in limestone
LF	
R	Singh 1979, 82
N	Mound locally called Ghuskari

168. Takhawan or Takhwan	
L	27°24′ N, 78°17′ E
T	Mound: 160 × 130 m, 8 m high
C	PGW cult., NBPW cult., Kushan period
D	Sherds: PGW, GW, BPW, RW, cSW, RSW Copper coin (Kushan) Brickbats

LF	
R	*IAR* 1960-1, 66 Tripathi 1976, 130 Singh 1979, 28 Shrimali 1983, vol. I, 202 Singh 1984 ?, 3 Roy 1986, xvii Ghosh 1989, vol. 2, 428
N	Fine grey dishes comparable with those of Hastinapura P. III

169. Thana Darioganj or Thana Danogaṇj	
L	27°37′24″ N, 79°04′07″ E
T	Mound: 100 × 100 m, 5 m high Temple Fort
C	Late Historical P.; Mughal period
D	• Mound: Sherds Terracotta figurines (Gurjara-Pratihara) Hindu sculptures (Gurjara-Pratihara) Brickbats • Temple square in plan, in limestone, erected over a basement 9 m² (medieval) • Fort: Remains of four corner towers, in *lakhauri* bricks, originally surrounded by a rampart in mud bricks
LF	
R	*IAR* 1960-1, 66 Singh 1979, 49-50 Singh 1984 ?, 10
N	Fort built by Khan Bahadur (eighteenth century AD)

170. Tharauli	
L	27°27′ N, 78°51′ E
T	Mound 1: 100 × 95 m, 6 m high Mound 2: 30 × 15 m, 1 m high
C	Late Historical P.
D	• Mound 1: Sherds: BPW, RW, BRW Votive tablets Hindu sculptures Bricks (38 × 21.5 × 7.5 cm) Remains of foundation walls • Mound 2: Sherds
LF	
R	Singh 1979, 74
N	Mound 2 known by the name of Dusasana

171. Timarna or Siroman Timarna or Timarua	
L	
T	Mound
C	PGW cult., NBPW cult.
D	Sherds: PGW, GW, BPW, bSW, RSW, RW Brickbats
LF	
R	*IAR* 1960-1, 66 Tripathi 1976, 131 Shrimali 1983, vol. I, 202 Singh 1984 ?, 3 Ghosh 1989, vol. 2, 440
N	

172. Trilokpur	
L	27°43′ N, 78°32′ E
T	Mound (small) Temple
C	Late Historical P.
D	Ruined temple with plinth and foundation in limestone Hindu sculptures
LF	Some sculptures located in the site locally known as Pathwari
R	Singh 1979, 81
N	

173. Tumaria	
L	27°54′ N, 78°48′ E Mound, east of village
T	Mound: 30 m², 2 m high
C	Late Historical P.
D	Sherds
LF	
R	Singh 1979, 88
N	Traditionally ascribed as a *garhi*

174. Ubhai Asadnagar	
L	27°24′24″ N, 79°12′14″ E
T	Mound: 60 × 50 m, 6 m high
C	Late Historical P.
D	Sherds: GW, RW, BSW, BPW Brickbats

LF	
R	Singh 1979, 100
N	

175. Umargarh or Gone-Umargarh	
L	27°32′01″ N, 78°21′18″ E
T	Mound: 300 × 130 m, 9 m high Forts
C	PGW cult., NBPW cult., Late Historical P.
D	Decorated pieces and Hindu sculptures (Gurjara-Pratihara) • Mound: Sherds: PGW, NBPW, BPW, BSW, GW, GRW, GBW, BRW, RPW Terracotta discs • Forts: Remains of four towers in the west fringe of mound, with a probably moat Similar fort did exist on the east side of mound
LF	
R	*IAR* 1960-1, 66 Tripathi 1976, 126 Singh 1979, 29-30 Shrimali 1983, vol. I, 197 Singh 1984 ?, 3 Roy 1986, xvii Ghosh 1989, vol. 2, 153 Chakrabarti et al. 2002, 116
N	

176. Wazirpur	
L	27°46′30″ N, 78°04′ E
T	Mound: 130 × 70 m, 6 m high Wells
C	Late Historical P.
D	• Mound: Sherds: GW, BPW Few terracottas 3 copper coins (tribal or Pancala?) Remains of four towers of a mud-bricks *garhi* • Wells: 2 brick wells (bricks: 45.5 × 30.5 × 7.5 cm)
LF	
R	Singh 1979, 82-3 Singh 1984 ?, 6
N	

177. Yagdarpur	
L	27°46′ N, 78°45′30″ E
T	Mound: 60 × 50 m, 2 m high
C	Late Historical P.
D	Sherds: RW, GW Brickbats
LF	
R	Singh 1979, 84
N	

ETAWAH DISTRICT

157 Sites

1. Aghar	
L	
T	
C	Late Historical P.
D	Sherds
LF	
R	*IAR* 1978-9, 22
N	

2. Aheripur	
L	*Tahsil* Bharthana
T	Temple
C	Late Historical P.
D	Remains not described
LF	
R	*IAR* 1987-8, 109
N	

3. Ahiran	
L	
T	
C	Late Historical P.

D	Sherds
LF	
R	*IAR* 1979-80, 76
N	

4. Airwa/Tikur	
L	26°53′35″ N, 79°25′18″ E
T	Mound: 8-10 acres, *c.* 18 m high Temple
C	Late Historical P.
D	Remains not described
LF	
R	*IAR* 1979-80, 76 Chakrabarti et al. 2002, 118
N	

5. Allahpur	
L	*Tahsil* Auraiya
T	
C	Late Historical P.
D	Sherds
LF	
R	*IAR* 1981-2, 70-1
N	

6. Anguthia	
L	*Tahsil* Auraiya
T	
C	NBPW cult.
D	Sherds: NBPW, GW
LF	
R	*IAR* 1981-2, 70-1
N	

7. Anison	
L	
T	
C	Late Historical P.
D	Sherds
LF	
R	*IAR* 1978-9, 22
N	

8. Asa	
L	
T	
C	Late Historical P.
D	Sherds
LF	
R	*IAR* 1979-80, 76
N	

9. Asai	
L	*Tahsil* Bharthana
T	
C	PGW cult., NBPW cult., Late Historical P.
D	Sherds: PGW, NBPW, RW Terracotta animal figurines Inscribed copper plate of Gaharwals (AD 1162) Remains of medieval structures
LF	
R	*IAR* 1969-70, 40 *IAR* 1975-6, 65 *IAR* 1987-8, 109
N	

10. Athesi	
L	
T	
C	Late Historical P.
D	Sherds
LF	
R	*IAR* 1978-9, 22
N	

11. Atsu	
L	26°35′19″ N, 79°21′06″ E
T	Mound: 8-10 acres, *c.* 4 m high
C	Early century AD

D	Finds not described
LF	
R	Chakrabarti et al. 2002, 118
N	

12. Ayana	
L	*Tahsil* Auraiya
T	
C	Sunga-Kushan period to Late Historical P.
D	Sherds: GW, RW
LF	
R	*IAR* 1985-6, 81
N	

13. Badshahpur-Chonk	
L	
T	
C	Late Historical P.
D	Sherds
LF	
R	*IAR* 1978-9, 22
N	

14. Bahadurpur Uncha	
L	
T	Temple

C	Late Historical P.
D	Brick-temple
LF	
R	*IAR* 1982-3, 96
N	

15. Baisauli	
L	26°42′07″ N, 79°23′34″ E
T	Mound: *c.* 10 acres, *c.* 8 m high
C	Early century AD
D	Finds not described
LF	
R	Chakrabarti et al. 2002, 118
N	

16. Bakewar	
L	*Tahsil* Bharthana
T	Temple
C	Late historical P.
D	Remains not described
LF	
R	*IAR* 1987-8, 109
N	

17. Balpur	
L	
T	
C	Late Historical P.
D	Sherds
LF	
R	*IAR* 1979-80, 76
N	

18. Balsauli	
L	
T	
C	Late Historical P.
D	Sherds
LF	
R	*IAR* 1979-80, 76
N	

19. Baralokpur	
L	26°55′54″ N, 79°10′27″ E
T	Mound: *c.* 20 acres, *c.* 20 m high
C	Early century AD
D	Sherds: BRW (?)
LF	
R	Chakrabarti et al. 2002, 117-18
N	

20. Barauna Khurd	
L	
T	
C	PGW cult., NBPW cult., Early Historical P., Late Historical P.
D	Sherds: PGW, NBPW, Sunga-Kushan, others (?)
LF	
R	*IAR* 1979-80, 76
N	

21. Barhan	
L	
T	
C	NBPW cult., Early Historical P., Late Historical P.
D	Sherds: NBPW, Sunga-Kushan, others (?)
LF	
R	*IAR* 1979-80, 76
N	

22. Barkasi	
L	
T	
C	Early Historical P., Late Historical P.
D	Finds not described
LF	
R	*IAR* 1978-9, 22
N	

23. Barru Keolasar	
L	
T	
C	Late Historical P.
D	Sherds
LF	
R	*IAR* 1978-9, 22
N	

24. Bela	
L	*Tahsil* Etawah
T	
C	Early Historical P., Late Historical P.
D	Finds not described
LF	
R	*IAR* 1978-9, 22 *IAR* 1988-9, 84
N	

25. Bhadaura	
L	
T	
C	Early Historical P., Late Historical P.
D	Sherds
LF	
R	*IAR* 1978-9, 22
N	

26. Bhadsan	
L	26°37′08″ N, 79°18′08″ E
T	Mound: *c.* 12 acres, *c.* 8 m high
C	Early century AD
D	Finds not described
LF	
R	Chakrabarti et al. 2002, 118
N	

27. Bhainsauri	
L	
T	
C	Early Historical P., Late Historical P.
D	Finds not described
LF	
R	*IAR* 1978-9, 22
N	

28. Bhararpura	
L	26°56′14″ N, 79°12′43″ E
T	Mound: *c.* 10 acres, *c.* 15 m high
C	Early Historical P.
D	Sherds: BRW
LF	
R	Chakrabarti et al. 2002, 117
N	

29. Bhasaura	
L	
T	
C	Early Historical P., Late Historical P.
D	Sherds
LF	
R	*IAR* 1979-80, 76
N	

30. Bhatauli	
L	
T	
C	Late Historical P.
D	Sherds
LF	
R	*IAR* 1978-9, 22
N	

31. Bhitragaon	
L	
T	
C	Late Historical P.
D	Sherds
LF	
R	*IAR* 1978-9, 22
N	

32. Bidhuna Taluk	
L	26°48′15″ N, 79°31′04″ E; west bank of the Rind
T	Mound: *c.* 20 acres, *c.* 14 m high
C	PGW cult., NBPW cult., Early century AD
D	Sherds: PGW, NBPW and associated wares
LF	
R	*IAR* 1978-9, 22 Chakrabarti et al. 2002, 118
N	

33. Bikapur	
L	
T	
C	NBPW cult., Early Historical P., Late Historical P.
D	Sherds
LF	
R	*IAR* 1979-80, 76
N	

34. Bilawa	
L	26°33′10″ N, 79°20′52″ E
T	Mound: *c.* 1 acre, *c.* 1.5 m high
C	Early century AD
D	Finds not described
LF	

R	Chakrabarti et al. 2002, 118
N	

35. Bina	
L	26°58′26″ N, 79°09′16″ E
T	Mound: *c.* 5 acres, *c.* 18 m high
C	Kushan period
D	Brickstructures
LF	
R	Chakrabarti et al. 2002, 117
N	

36. Birhuni	
L	26°34′01″ N, 79°22′45″ E
T	Mound: *c.* 1 acre, *c.* 2 m high
C	Early century AD
D	Finds not described
LF	
R	Chakrabarti et al. 2002, 118
N	

37. Burru Phaphund	
L	
T	
C	PGW cult., NBPW cult., Early Historical P., Late Historical P.

D	Sherds: PGW, NBPW, Sunga-Kushan, others (?)
LF	
R	*IAR* 1979-80, 76
N	

38. Chakannagar Kheda or Chakranagar or Chakarnagar or Sagre	
L	26°34′49″ N, 79°05′39″ E, *Tahsil* Bharthana
T	*Khera c.* 3 miles in circuit
C	PGW cult., NBPW cult., Early century AD
D	Sherds: PGW, BRW, BSW, NBPW, RW Terracotta figurines (early century AD)
LF	
R	*IAR* 1969-70, 40 *IAR* 1987-8, 109 Dey 1927, 59 Shrimali 1983, vol. I, 196 Roy 1986, xvii Ghosh 1989, vol. 2, 92 Chakrabarti 1997, 192, 251 Chakrabarti et al. 2002, 118
N	Identified with Chakranagara (and with Ekachakra) of *Mahabharata*

39. Chakarpur	
L	
T	
C	Late Historical P.
D	Sherds

LF	
R	*IAR* 1979-80, 76
N	

40. Chakwabuzurg	
L	*Tahsil* Etawah
T	Temple
C	Late Historical P.
D	Remains not described
LF	
R	*IAR* 1987-8, 109
N	

41. Chamkani	
L	
T	
C	Late Historical P.
D	Sherds
LF	
R	*IAR* 1979-80, 76
N	

42. Chapta	
L	
T	
C	Late Historical P.

D	Sherds: GW, RW
LF	
R	*IAR* 1982-3, 96
N	

43. Chhachund or Chhachhund	
L	26°41′43″ N, 79°22′31″ E
T	Mound: *c.* 3 acres, *c.* 6 m high
C	Late Historical P.
D	Sherds
LF	
R	*IAR* 1979-80, 76 Chakrabarti et al. 2002, 118
N	

44. Chirahaulia	
L	*Tahsil* Auraiya
T	
C	Late Historical P.
D	Sherds
LF	
R	*IAR* 1981-2, 70-1
N	

45. Dakhnai	
L	
T	
C	Late Historical P.
D	Sherds
LF	
R	*IAR* 1979-80, 76
N	

46. Damarpur	
L	
T	
C	Late Historical P.
D	Sherds
LF	
R	*IAR* 1978-9, 22
N	

47. Deokali	
L	26°25′56″ N, 79°29′36″ E
T	
C	Kushan period, Late Historical P.
D	Bricks
LF	
R	Chakrabarti et al. 2002, 119
N	

48. Dhorhra	
L	
T	
C	Late Historical P.
D	Sherds
LF	
R	*IAR* 1978-9, 22
N	

49. Dobah	
L	
T	
C	NBPW cult., Early Historical P., Late Historical P.
D	Sherds: NBPW, Sunga-Kushan, others (?)
LF	
R	*IAR* 1979-80, 76
N	

50. Dugaoli	
L	*Tahsil* Etawah
T	Temple
C	Late Historical P.
D	Remains not described
LF	
R	*IAR* 1987-8, 109
N	

51. Etawah	
L	
T	Mound (fort ?)
C	NBPW cult., Late Historical P.
D	Sherds: NBPW, others (?) Terracotta animal figurines
LF	
R	*IAR* 1962-3, 54 *IAR* 1969-70, 40 *IAR* 1988-9, 84 Shrimali 1983, vol. I, 197 Roy 1986, xvii Ghosh 1989, vol. 2, 137
N	Sanskrit inscription in *nagari* characters (thirteenth century AD) Islamic tomb

52. Fapkapur	
L	
T	
C	Late Historical P.
D	Sherds
LF	
R	*IAR* 1979-80, 76
N	

53. Fatehpur	
L	
T	
C	Late Historical P.
D	Sherds
LF	
R	*IAR* 1978-9, 22
N	

54. Goanri	
L	
T	Fort
C	NBPW cult., Early Historical P., Late Historical P.
D	Sherds: NBPW, Sunga-Kushan, others (?) Remains of a fortress
LF	
R	*IAR* 1979-80, 76
N	

55. Gura	
L	
T	
C	Late Historical P.
D	Sherds
LF	
R	*IAR* 1979-80, 76
N	

56. Harchandpur	
L	
T	
C	Early Historical P., Late Historical P.
D	Sherds
LF	
R	*IAR* 1979-80, 76
N	

57. Hardu	
L	
T	
C	Late Historical P.
D	Sherds
LF	
R	*IAR* 1978-9, 22
N	

58. Hasanpur	
L	
T	
C	Late Historical P.
D	Sherds
LF	
R	*IAR* 1979-80, 76
N	

59. Hoheri	
L	*Tahsil* Auriya
T	
C	Early Historical P., Late Historical P.
D	Sherds: GRW, RW, mica dusted pottery Terracotta lamp fragment
LF	
R	*IAR* 1984-5, 88-9
N	

60. Jauhar	
L	
T	
C	Late Historical P.
D	Sherds
LF	
R	*IAR* 1978-9, 22
N	

61. Jaunra	
L	
T	
C	Late Historical P.
D	Sherds: BSW, others (?)
LF	
R	*IAR* 1983-4, 88
N	

62. Jiraon	
L	
T	
C	Late Historical P.
D	Sherds
LF	
R	*IAR* 1979-80, 76
N	

63. Jiva Sirsani Parsu	
L	
T	
C	Late Historical P.
D	Sherds
LF	
R	*IAR* 1978-9, 22
N	

64. Jua	
L	*Tahsil* Auraiya
T	
C	Late Historical P.
D	Sherds
LF	
R	*IAR* 1981-2, 70-1
N	

65. Juhikha	
L	*Tahsil* Auraiya
T	
C	Sunga-Kushan period to Late Historical P.
D	Sherds: GW, RW
LF	
R	*IAR* 1985-6, 81
N	

66. Kakor-Khurd	
L	*Tahsil* Auraiya
T	
C	Late Historical P.
D	Sherds
LF	
R	*IAR* 1981-2, 70-1
N	

67. Kanauli	
L	
T	
C	Late Historical P.
D	Sherds
LF	
R	*IAR* 1978-9, 22
N	

68. Kanmau	
L	
T	
C	Late Historical P.
D	Sherds
LF	
R	*IAR* 1978-9, 22
N	

69. Karauli	
L	
T	
C	Gupta period, Ninth century AD
D	Hindu sculpture (Gupta) *Nagari* inscription (Ninth century AD)
LF	
R	*IAR* 1978-9, 22
N	

70. Karri	
L	26°57′57″ N, 79°11′19″ E
T	Mound: *c.* 10 acres, *c.* 12 m high
C	Early century AD
D	Brickbats
LF	
R	Chakrabarti et al. 2002, 117
N	

71. Khanpur	
L	*Tahsil* Auraiya
T	Temple
C	Late Historical P.
D	Remains not described
LF	
R	*IAR* 1981-2, 70-1
N	

72. Kheda Jaychand	
L	
T	
C	Late Historical P.
D	Terracotta animal figurines Remains of structures
LF	
R	*IAR* 1969-70, 40
N	

73. Kheola	
L	*Tahsil* Auraiya
T	Temple
C	Late Historical P.
D	Remains not described
LF	
R	*IAR* 1981-2, 70-1
N	

74. Kudarkot	
L	26°48′34″ N, 79°23′23″ E; south of Puroha Nadi
T	Mound: 80-5 acres, *c.* 18 m high Temple
C	PGW cult., NBPW cult., Early Historical P., Late Historical P.
D	• Mound: Sherds: PGW, BSW, NBPW, Sunga-Kushan, others (?) Brickbats • Temple (medieval) in ruins
LF	
R	*IAR* 1979-80, 76 Chakrabarti et al. 2002, 118
N	

75. Kueta	
L	26°56′24″ N, 79°15′10″ E
T	Mound: *c.* 6 acres, *c.* 7 m high
C	Early century AD
D	Finds not described
LF	
R	Chakrabarti et al. 2002, 118
N	

76. Kurkha	
L	*Tahsil* Bharthana
T	Mound Temple

C	Late Historical P.
D	• Mound: Sherds: RW, BSW
LF	
R	*IAR* 1986-7, 78
N	

77. Kursi	
L	
T	
C	Late Historical P.
D	Sherds
LF	
R	*IAR* 1978-9, 22
N	

78. Ladhaura	
L	
T	
C	Late Historical P.
D	Sherds
LF	
R	*IAR* 1979-80, 76
N	

79. Lakhi	
L	
T	
C	Late Historical P.
D	Sherds
LF	
R	*IAR* 1978-9, 22
N	

80. Lakhna	
L	*Tahsil* Bharthana
T	Temple
C	Late Historical P.
D	
LF	
R	*IAR* 1987-8, 109
N	

81. Lakhnu	
L	
T	
C	Late Historical P.
D	Sherds
LF	
R	*IAR* 1978-9, 22
N	

82. Laungpur	
L	*Tahsil* Etawah
T	Temple
C	Late Historical P.
D	Remains not described
LF	
R	*IAR* 1987-8, 109
N	

83. Madhuapur	
L	
T	
C	Early Historical P., Late Historical P.
D	Finds not described Temple (medieval)
LF	
R	*IAR* 1978-9, 22
N	

84. Madhuapur (Garhi)	
L	
T	
C	Early Historical P., Late Historical P.
D	Finds not described
LF	
R	*IAR* 1978-9, 22
N	

85. Madrai Jakh	
L	
T	
C	Late Historical P.
D	Sherds
LF	
R	*IAR* 1979-80, 76
N	

86. Maharajpur	
L	*Tahsil* Etawah
T	Temple
C	Late Historical P.
D	Remains not described
LF	
R	*IAR* 1988-9, 84
N	

87. Mahewa	
L	*Tahsil* Bharthana
T	Temple
C	Late Historical P.
D	Remains not described
LF	
R	*IAR* 1987-8, 109
N	

88. Malhausi	
L	
T	
C	NBPW cult.
D	Sherds: NBPW, BSW, GW
LF	
R	*IAR* 1978-9, 22
N	

89. Mamen or Maman	
L	26°52′07″ N, 79°16′48″ E; *tahsil* Bharthana; S bank of Puroha Nadi
T	Mound: *c.* 25 acres, *c.* 12 m high
C	PGW cult., NBPW cult., Early century AD
D	Sherds: PGW, NBPW, BSW, RW Brickbats
LF	
R	*IAR* 1987-8, 109 Chakrabarti et al. 2002, 118
N	

90. Manakpur Bisu	
L	*Tahsil* Etawah
T	Temple
C	Late Historical P.
D	Remains not described

LF	
R	*IAR* 1988-9, 84
N	

91. Marokha	
L	
T	
C	Late Hstorical P.
D	Sherds
LF	
R	*IAR* 1978-9, 22
N	

92. Mathaipur	
L	*Tahsil* Auraiya
T	Temple
C	Late Historical P.
D	Remains not described
LF	
R	*IAR* 1981-2, 70-1
N	

93. Mau	
L	
T	
C	Late Historical P.

D	Sherds
LF	
R	*IAR* 1979-80, 76
N	

94. Milk Husainpur Kalan	
L	*Tahsil* Auraiya
T	
C	NBPW cult., Late Historical P.
D	Sherds
LF	
R	*IAR* 1981-2, 70-1
N	

95. Modena-Rampatta	
L	*Tahsil* Auraiya
T	
C	Late Historical P.
D	Sherds
LF	
R	*IAR* 1981-2, 70-1
N	

96. Mohri	
L	26°57′03″ N, 79°17′10″ E; *tahsil* Bharthana
T	Mound: *c.* 10 acres, 7-8 m high

C	Sunga-Kushan period, Late Historical P.
D	Sherds: RW, GW
LF	
R	*IAR* 1986-7, 78 Chakrabarti et al. 2002, 118
N	

97. Munj	
L	26°53′49″ N, 79°09′21″ E; *tahsil* Etawah; E bank of Ahneya Nadi
T	Mound: 25-30 acres, *c.* 30 m high
C	PGW cult., NBPW cult., Early century AD
D	Sherds Brickbats
LF	
R	*IAR* 1988-9, 84 Chakrabarti et al. 2002, 118
N	

98. Murha Chhadamilal	
L	
T	
C	Late Historical P.
D	Sherds
LF	
R	*IAR* 1978-9, 22
N	

99. Nagaria	
L	
T	
C	PGW cult., NBPW cult., Early Historical P., Late Historical P.
D	Sherds
LF	
R	*IAR* 1979-80, 76
N	

100. Narayanpur	
L	*Tahsil* Auraiya
T	
C	Late Historical P.
D	Sherds: RW, GW Dabber
LF	
R	*IAR* 1984-5, 88
N	

101. Narha	
L	
T	
C	Late Historical P.
D	Sherds
LF	

R	*IAR* 1979-80, 76
N	

102. Naugaon	
L	
T	
C	Early Historical P., Late Historical P.
D	Sherds
LF	
R	*IAR* 1979-80, 76
N	

103. Nawada Mamrezpur	
L	
T	Temple
C	Late Historical P.
D	Brick temple
LF	
R	*IAR* 1982-3, 96
N	

104. Newari Kalan	
L	26°39′52″ N, 79°17′09″ E
T	Mound: *c.* 10 acres, *c.* 8 m high
C	Early century AD
D	Finds not described

LF	
R	Chakrabarti et al. 2002, 118
N	

105. Niorai	
L	
T	
C	Undated
D	Copper Hoard
LF	
R	Ghosh 1989, vol. 2, 317-18
N	

106. Niwari Khurd	
L	26°38′36″ N, 79°16′48″ E
T	Mound: *c.* 5 acres, *c.* 8 m high
C	Early century AD
D	Finds not described
LF	
R	Chakrabarti et al. 2002, 118
N	

107. Oron	
L	
T	
C	Late Historical P.

D	Sherds
LF	
R	*IAR* 1978-9, 22
N	

108. Otaun	
L	
T	
C	Late Historical P.
D	Sherds
LF	
R	*IAR* 1979-80, 76
N	

109. Pachdeora	
L	*Tahsil* Etawah
T	Temple
C	Late Historical P.
D	Remains not described
LF	
R	*IAR* 1987-8, 109
N	

110. Pachhian Geon	
L	*Tahsil* Etawah
T	Temple

C	Late Historical P.
D	Remains not described
LF	
R	*IAR* 1988-9, 84
N	

111. Pakhangoi	
L	
T	
C	Early Historical P., Late Historical P.
D	Sherds
LF	
R	*IAR* 1979-80, 76
N	

112. Palia	
L	
T	
C	Late Historical P.
D	Sherds
LF	
R	*IAR* 1978-9, 22
N	

113. Passaipur-Kashampur	
L	*Tahsil* Auraiya
T	
C	Late Historical P.
D	Sherds
LF	
R	*IAR* 1981-2, 70-1
N	

114. Passauli	
L	
T	
C	Late Historical P.
D	Sherds
LF	
R	*IAR* 1978-9, 22
N	

115. Pasua	
L	
T	
C	Early Historical P., Late Historical P.
D	Sherds
LF	
R	*IAR* 1979-80, 76
N	

116. Patti Nam	
L	
T	Temple
C	Late Historical P.
D	Brick temple
LF	
R	*IAR* 1982-3, 96
N	

117. Patti Yaqubpur	
L	
T	
C	Early Historical P., Late Historical P.
D	Finds not described
LF	
R	*IAR* 1978-9, 22
N	

118. Pertalner	
L	*Tahsil* Etawah
T	Fort
C	Late Hstorical P.
D	Remains not described
LF	
R	*IAR* 1988-9, 84
N	

119. Phaphund	
L	26°35′54″ N, 79°27′40″ E
T	Mound: *c.* 2 acres, *c.* 2 m high
C	Early century AD, Late Historical P.
D	Sherds
LF	
R	*IAR* 1978-9, 22 Chakrabarti et al. 2002, 118
N	

120. Phulpur	
L	26°34′36″ N, 79°15′51″ E
T	Mound: *c.* 1 acre, *c.* 1 m high
C	Late Historical P.
D	Finds not described
LF	
R	Chakrabarti et al. 2002, 118
N	

121. Piprauli Sheo	
L	
T	
C	Late Historical P.
D	Sherds
LF	
R	*IAR* 1978-9, 22
N	

122. Pirthi Rampur	
L	*Tahsil* Bharthana
T	
C	Undated
D	Sherds: BSW, RW
LF	
R	*IAR* 1987-8, 109
N	

123. Ponthi	
L	
T	
C	Late Historical P.
D	Sherds
LF	
R	*IAR* 1978-9, 22
N	

124. Purwa Mana	
L	
T	
C	Late Historical P.
D	Sherds
LF	
R	*IAR* 1978-9, 22
N	

125. Qasba Babarpur	
L	26°34′26″ N, 79°18′35″ E
T	Mound: *c.* 1 acre, *c.* 1.5 m high
C	Sunga period
D	Sherds
LF	
R	Chakrabarti et al. 2002, 118
N	

126. Qasba Janan	
L	26°30′58″ N, 78°23′08″ E
T	Mound: *c.* 10 acres, *c.* 5 m high
C	Second century BC
D	Finds not described
LF	
R	Chakrabarti et al. 2002, 119
N	

127. Qasba Shinganpur	
L	*Tahsil* Auraiya
T	
C	Sunga-Kushan period to Late Historical P.
D	Sherds: GW, RW
LF	
R	*IAR* 1985-6, 81
N	

128. Rampur Behari	
L	*Tahsil* Auraiya
T	
C	Late Historical P.
D	Sherds
LF	
R	*IAR* 1981-2, 70-1
N	

129. Rataur	
L	*Tahsil* Bharthana
T	Temple
C	Late Historical P.
D	Remains not described
LF	
R	*IAR* 1987-8, 109
N	

130. Ratuwa	
L	*Tahsil* Auraiya
T	
C	Late Historical P.
D	Sherds
LF	
R	*IAR* 1981-2, 70-1
N	

131. Roshangpur	
L	26°29′38″ N, 79°22′51″ E
T	Mound: *c.* 5 acres, *c.* 1 m high
C	Early century AD
D	Finds not described
LF	
R	Chakrabarti et al. 2002, 118-19
N	

132. Rurukalan	
L	26°45′25″ N, 79°27′49″ E
T	Mound: *c.* 25 acres, *c.* 13 m high
C	NBPW cult., Early Historical P., Late Historical P.
D	Sherds: NBPW, Sunga-Kushan, others (?)
LF	
R	*IAR* 1979-80, 76 Chakrabarti et al. 2002, 118
N	

133. Rurukhurd	
L	
T	
C	Late Historical P.
D	Sherds
LF	
R	*IAR* 1979-80, 76
N	

134. Sabhad	
L	
T	
C	NBPW cult., Early Historical P., Late Historical P..
D	Sherds: NBPW, Sunga-Kushan, others (?)
LF	
R	*IAR* 1979-80, 76
N	

135. Sahar	
L	26°45′30″ N, 79°35′37″ E
T	Mound
C	NBPW cult., Early century AD
D	Sherds: NBPW, BSW, GW
LF	
R	*IAR* 1978-9, 22 Chakrabarti et al. 2002, 118
N	

136. Sainfi	
L	*Tahsil* Bharthana
T	Mound
C	NBPW cult.
D	Sherds: NBPW, BSW, RW
LF	
R	*IAR* 1986-7, 78
N	

137. Saipai or Saifai Lichchwai	excavated
L	26°27′ N, 78°58′ E
L	
C	OCP cult.
D	Sherds: OCP, RW Sandstone querns, pounders, pellets, balls Chalcedony flake Bone fragments Pieces of kiln-burnt clay Reed impression on lumps of clay (wattle-and-daub construction) Copper Hoard
LF	
R	*IAR* 1969-70, 40 *IAR* 1970-1, 38 *IAR* 1971-2, 46-7 Dikshit 1979, 127, 287, 296 Shrimali 1983, vol. I, 201 Possehl 1986, 88-9 Ghosh 1989, vol. 2, 384 Dhavalikar 1997, 268-9
N	

138. Saken	
L	26°22′28″ N, 79°37′28″ E
T	Mound: *c.* 10 acres, *c.* 10 m high
C	NBPW cult., Sunga period
D	Sherds
LF	

R	Chakrabarti et al. 2002, 119
N	

139. Salaiya	
L	*Tahsil* Auraiya
T	
C	Late Historical P.
D	Sherds
LF	
R	*IAR* 1981-2, 70-1
N	

140. Samain	
L	
T	
C	PGW cult., NBPW cult., Early Historical P., Late Historical P.
D	Sherds: PGW, NBPW, Sunga-Kushan, others (?)
LF	
R	*IAR* 1979-80, 76
N	

141. Sampar	
L	26°37′08″ N, 79°20′09″ E
T	Mound: *c.* 6 acres, *c.* 15 m high
C	NBPW cult., Sunga period, Early century AD

D	Sherds
LF	
R	Chakrabarti et al. 2002, 118
N	

142. Santokhpur Ghat	
L	*Tahsil* Etawah
T	
C	PGW cult., NBPW cult.
D	Sherds
LF	
R	*IAR* 1988-9, 84
N	

143. Sarai Ajitmal	
L	26°33′35″ N, 79°18′00″ E
T	Mound: *c.* 1 acre, *c.* 1 m high
C	Early century AD
D	Finds not described
LF	
R	Chakrabarti et al. 2002, 118
N	

144. Sarai Anantram	
L	26°36′20″ N, 79°15′24″ E
T	Mound: *c.* 1 acre

C	Late Historical P.
D	Finds not described
LF	
R	Chakrabarti et al. 2002, 118
N	

145. Sarsai Helu	
L	26°59′44″ N, 79°10′48″ E; *tahsil* Etawah
T	Mound: *c.* 12 acres, *c.* 15 m high
C	Early century AD
D	Sherds: GW, RW, BSW (?)
LF	
R	*IAR* 1988-9, 84 Chakrabarti et al. 2002, 117
N	

146. Sarsainagar	
L	*Tahsil* Bharthana
T	Temple
C	Late Historical P.
D	Remains not described
LF	
R	*IAR* 1987-8, 109
N	

147. Sarsai Nawar	
L	26°57′37″ N, 79°14′10″ E
T	Mound: 6-7 acres, *c.* 13 m high
C	Early century AD
D	Brickbats
LF	
R	Chakrabarti et al. 2002, 118
N	

148. Saunthra	
L	26°42′30″ N, 79°35′28″ E; east bank of the Rind River
T	Mound: *c.* 10 acres, *c.* 3 m high
C	NBPW cult., Early century AD
D	Sherds: NBPW, BSW, GW
LF	
R	*IAR* 1978-9, 22 Chakrabarti et al. 2002, 118
N	

149. Sehud	
L	26°36′14″ N, 79°33′41″ E
T	Mound: *c.* 10 acres, *c.* 9 m high
C	Kushan period, Gupta period
D	Bricks
LF	
R	Chakrabarti et al. 2002, 118
N	

150. Shabbadian	
L	
T	
C	Late Historical P.
D	Sherds: RW
LF	
R	*IAR* 1983-4, 88
N	

151. Shahpur	
L	
T	
C	Late Historical P.
D	Sherds
LF	
R	*IAR* 1979-80, 76
N	

152. Siunj	
L	
T	
C	Late Historical P.
D	Sherds
LF	
R	*IAR* 1978-9, 22
N	

153. Tajpur Phaphund	
L	
T	
C	Late Historical P.
D	Sherds
LF	
R	*IAR* 1978-9, 22
N	

154. Tirkhi	
L	26°57′24″ N, 79°12′02″ E
T	Mound: *c.* 2 acres, c. 10 m high
C	Early century AD
D	Finds not described
LF	
R	Chakrabarti et al. 2002, 117
N	

155. Ujhani	
L	*Tahsil* Bharthana
T	Temple
C	Late Historical P.
D	Remains not described
LF	
R	*IAR* 1987-8, 109
N	

156. Umrai	
L	*Tahsil* Etawah
T	Temple
C	Late Historical P.
D	Remains not described
LF	
R	*IAR* 1987-8, 109
N	

157. Umrain	
L	
T	
C	Early Historical P., Late Historical P.
D	Sherds
LF	
R	*IAR* 1979-80, 76
N	

FARRUKHABAD DISTRICT

37 Sites

1. Amirpur or Amritpur	
L	22 km north of Fatehgarh
T	Fort
C	Late Historical P.
D	Remains not described
LF	
R	Singh 1979, 107 Paul 1985, 54
N	

2. Baḫua	
L	
T	
C	NBPW cult.
D	Sherds
LF	
R	Shrimali 1983, vol. I, 196
N	

3. Baraun	
L	27°24′35″ N, 79°30′23″ E
T	Mound: *c.* 4 ha, *c.* 3 m high

C	Early century AD
D	Sherds: BSW Brickbats
LF	
R	Chakrabarti et al. 2002, 115
N	

4. Bhojpur

L	27°17′ N, 79°41′ east; 10 km south of Fatehgarh
T	Fort
C	Late Historical P. (Medieval phase), Thirteenth century AD
D	Remains of fortification
LF	
R	Singh 1979, 107 Paul 1985, 59-60
N	Fort erected by Raja Bhoja of Malwa Site identified with Bhojakata, mentioned in the *Ṣkanda Purana* A stone figure of a couchant lion (second century AD) has been noticed

5. Bishungarh or Bishangarh

L	27°10′ N, 79°35′ E; 53 km south-west of Fatehgarh
T	Fort
C	Late Historical P.
D	Fort enclosed within wall and dich
LF	

R	Singh 1979, 107 Paul 1985, 61
N	

6. Chaudhariapur	
L	2.5 km east of Kanauj
T	
C	Eighth-ninth century AD
D	Numerous Hindu sculptures
LF	
R	Paul 1985, 62
N	

7. Chhibramau	
L	27 km south-west of Fatehgarh
T	Fort
C	Late Historical P. (Medieval phase)
D	Ruined fort
LF	
R	Singh 1979, 107 Paul 1985, 63
N	

8. Devakali	
L	3 km east of Kanauj
T	

C	Eighth-tenth century AD
D	Numerous Hindu sculptures Architectural fragments
LF	
R	Paul 1985, 63
N	

9. Dhilawal	
L	27°22′16″ N, 79°34′30″ E
T	Mound: *c.* 1.5 ha, *c.* 1.5 m high
C	Early century AD
D	Sherds
LF	
R	Chakrabarti et al. 2002, 116
N	

10. Drupad Kila	
L	27°36′20″ N, 79°17′30″ E, 6 km south-west of Kampil Mound 1, Jhinjauta village Mounds 2, 3, 4, 5, 6, north-north-west outside walls Mound 7, E outside walls
T	Mounds Town-walls: 830 × 683 m, rectangular
C	Sunga-Kushan period, Late Historical P.
D	• Inside the walls: Sherds: GW, RW Terracotta finds: balls, spindle whorls, broken animal figurines, votive object with inclusion and inscription, architectural fragments

	Stone structural members Pancala coin Bricks (34.5-35.5 × 24-25 × 4-4.5 cm, 31 × 21 × 5 cm) Remains of structural activity • Mounds: Sherds: GW, RW Brickbats Remains of structural activity
LF	
R	Dallaporta, Marcato 1999, 31-64; 2001, 161-9 Dikshit 2000, 164-72
N	See Jhinjhauta Buzurg and Paharpur in Chakrabarti et al. 2002, 115.

11. Farrukhabad	
L	27°24′ N, 79°40′ E Mound west of town
T	Mound: 20 m high Walls surround the city
C	PGW cult., NBPW cult., Late Historical P.
D	• Mound: Sherds: PGW, RW, BPW, BRW Terracotta incised discs, broken figurine Gold coin of king Harsha (Seventh century AD) Buddha statue • Walls: Remains of triangular embankment with flanking towers
LF	Buddha statue collected in the Bharata Kala Bhavan of Varanasi

R	*IAR* 1955-6, 71 *IAR* 1965-6, 47 Tripathi 1976, 125 Singh 1979, 104 Shrimali 1983, vol. I, 196 Paul 1985, 63-4 Roy 1986, xviii Ghosh 1989, vol. 2, 73, 138
N	Mound locally called Bhishmapur connected with Draupadi A mud fort flanked by bastions, surrounded by a ditch was built by Nawab Muhammad: there was a palace called Bara Mahal and a Jami Masjid (both ruined) Terracotta incised discs comparable with those of Hastinapura

12. Fatehgarh	
L	27°22′ N, 79°38′ E
T	
C	
D	Copper Hoard
LF	
R	Paul 1985, 64-5 Ghosh 1989, vol. 2, 138
N	There is a mud fort (eighteenth century AD)

13. Godhani	
L	12 km north-west of Kanauj
T	
C	Seventh-tenth century AD

D	Hindu, Jaina sculptures Architectural fragments
LF	
R	Paul 1985, 65
N	

14. Jankhat	
L	26°53′ N, 79°51′ E; 28 km south-west of Kanauj
T	Mound
C	Late Historical P.
D	Sherds Fragmentary stone sculptures Stone inscription (Thirteenth century AD) Brickbats
LF	
R	Paul 1985, 68
N	Inscription of king Virasena Traditionally the site is connected with King Janaka of Mithila

15. Jaunra	
L	27°33′ N, 79°18′ E; 3 km from Kaimganj Mound, 1 km south of village
T	Mound: 200 × 100 m
C	Second century BC to Eleventh century AD
D	Sherds: BSW, GW, RW
LF	

R	
N	Personal observations (Dallaporta, Marcato) Local tradition: site of a Chauhan fort

16. Kampil	excavated
L	27°36′ N, 79°16′ E; 39 km west of Farrukhabad Mound, north-west of village
T	Mound: 125 × 80 m, 8 m high Temples
C	PGW cult., NBPW cult. to Late Historical P.
D	• Mound: Sherds: PGW, RW, BPW, BRW, GW Terracotta human figurines (since Sunga period), incised discs Hindu, Jaina stone sculptures Architectural *kankar* members • Temples: Mahadeva temple in bricks and stone Some Jaina temples
LF	Some terracotta figurines and objects collected in BHU (Dept. of Ancient History, Culture and Archaeology), Varanasi Several sculptures and terracotta plaques preserved in the State Museum Lakhnau Numerous sculptures and fragments collected in the local Svetambar Temple
R	*AI* 10&11, 140, 144 *IAR* 1965-6, 48 *IAR* 1975-6, 51-2 *IAR* 1977-8, 70-1 Tripathi 1976, 31, 127 Singh 1979, 36-7

	Shrimali 1983, vol. I, 198 Roy 1983, 26 Paul 1985, 69-70 Roy 1986, 51-2, xix Possehl 1986, 48 Ghosh 1989, vol. 2, 198 Chakrabarti 1997, 191 Chakrabarti et al. 2002, 114
N	Mound locally called Draupadigarh Site identified with ancient Kampilya Several Muslim tombs Fort of Ghias-ad-din Balban (?)

17. Kanauj or **Kannauj**	excavated
L	27°03′ N, 79°59′ E Mound Club Ghar Tila near the hospital Other sites near Kannauj: Gwal Maidan, Shikhana Mound, Qila Mound, Lallan Miyan-ka-roja Fields W of the town, near the ancient riverbed
T	Mound (Club Ghar Tila): circumf. 200 m, 15/20 m high Palace Mosque Tombs
C	OCP cult., PGW cult., NBPW cult., Early Historical P., Late Historical P.; Sultanate, Mughal periods
D	• Mound: Sherds: BRW, PGW, NBPW, RW (Kushan), pottery of early century AD Terracotta finds: figurines (Sunga, Kushan, Gupta, medieval), discs, seals, *sati-sata* placque Brickbats • Area near the river (0.81 ha): Sherds: OCP (more frequent in the north part)

	Hindu stone sculpture (late-Kushan) Silver punch-marked, Kushan coins • Other sites: Sherds: PGW, NBPW, RW, BSW Terracotta figurines (Maurya, Sunga-Kushan, Gupta, medieval) Bone objects Hindu sculptures (Gurjara-Pratihara) Sanscrit inscription (tenth-eleventh century AD) Epigraphs (fifteenth century-seventeenth century AD) • Palace Rang Mahal (AD 1685) • Mosque Jami Masjid (AD 1406)
LF	Late-Kushan stone sculpture located on a pillar of a modern temple Sanskrit inscription on the pedestal of an image in Ajaypal temple
R	*IAR* 1955-6, 19-20 *IAR* 1963-4, 81, 82 *IAR* 1968-9, 70 *IAR* 1974-5, 45, 59 *IAR* 1978-9, 22, 101 *IAR* 1986-7, 123 Tripathi 1976, 31, 127 Singh 1979, 32-5, 107-8 Shrimali 1983, vol. I, 198 Roy 1983, 25-6 Paul 1985, 70-4 Possehl 1986, 48 Roy 1986, 48-9 Ghosh 1989, vol. 2, 199-200 Chakrabarti 1997, 191-2
N	Ancient Kanyakubja flourishing during Harsha's time Quoted by Chinese pilgrims Fa Hsien and Hsuan Tsang

18. Kanpatia or Kanpatiyapur	
L	6 km W of Kanauj
T	Mound
C	Late Historical P.
D	Sherds Hindu, Jaina stone sculptures Brickbats
LF	Some sculptures located in Murari Devi Temple Image of Mahavira with inscription (AD 1052) preserved in Archaeological Museum Kanauj
R	*IAR* 1974-5, 59 Paul 1985, 74
N	

19. Khairnagar	
L	26°06′ N, 79°50′ E, 9 km north-west of Jankhat
T	Mound Fort
C	Late Historical P.
D	Fort built in bricks over an old mound
LF	
R	Singh 1979, 104 Paul 1985, 75
N	Fort erected by Rotam Singh

20. Kutlupur	
L	1.5 km west of Kanauj
T	

C	Eighth-ninth century AD
D	Two stone sculptures
LF	Sculptures collected in the local temple of Rama-Lakshmana
R	Paul 1985, 76
N	

21. Mahmudpur Bija	
L	
T	
C	Fourth century AD, Gupta period
D	5 gold coins of Samudragupta
LF	Coins collected in the Police station of Kanauj
R	*IAR* 1986-7, 116
N	

22. Majhola	
L	27°32′08″ N, 79°19′17″ E
T	Mound: 1 m high
C	Late century BC, Early century AD
D	Sherds
LF	
R	Chakrabarti et al. 2002, 115
N	Small portion of mound around the spot called Baram Deo.

23. Makarand Nagar or Makrandnagar	
L	Mounds, south-east of village Pool, south-east of village
T	Mounds (three) Temple Pool
C	Late Historical P.; Sultanate, Mughal periods
D	• Mounds: Sherds Sculptures Brickbats • Temple (late medieval) • Pool (dried)
LF	
R	*IAR* 1978-9, 22 Singh 1979, 105
N	Pool called Suraj-kund

24. Masumpur	
L	
T	Mound
C	Late Historical P.
D	Sculptures Fragments of structural members
LF	
R	*IAR* 1974-5, 45
N	

25. Muhammadabad or Muhamadabad	
L	27°18′29″ N, 79°25′32″ E, 19 km south-west of Fatehgarh
T	Mound: *c.* 400 × 600 m, *c.*12 m high Fort or monastery
C	Kushan period (?), Late Historical P.
D	Fort or monastery erected on the old mound Traces of a few brick-built *stupas*
LF	
R	Singh 1979, 105 Paul 1985, 78 Chakrabarti et al. 2002, 115-16
N	Mound called Kal ka Khera

26. Pakhna Bihar or **Bihar**	
L	27°17′29″ N, 79°19′26″ E, 10 km east of Sankissa
T	Mound: 300/325 × 215 m
C	Kushan period, Tenth century AD
D	Sherds Terracotta inscribed seals, moulded terracottas Kushan inscription Buddhist rail-bars Large Buddha statue Carved bricks, brickbats
LF	
R	Singh 1979, 105 Paul 1985, 80-1 Chakrabarti et al. 2002, 115
N	Site of a famous Buddhist *vihara*, quoted by the pilgrim Hsuan Tsang

27. Pama	
L	
T	
C	NBPW cult.
D	Sherds
LF	
R	Shrimali 1983, vol. I, 200
N	

28. Pilkhana	
L	
T	Mound
C	Late Historical P.
D	Sherds Coins Sculptures
LF	
R	Singh 1979, 105
N	Identified by Fuhrer with ancient Pilo-shan-na, but Cunningham identified Pilo-shan-na with Bilsar

6. Rajgiri or Rajgir	
L	5 km south-east of Kanauj
T	Mound
C	Late Historical P.
D	Sherds Brickbats

LF	
R	*IAR* 1978-9, 22 Paul 1985, 82
N	

30. Salempur	
L	4 km south-east of Kanauj
T	
C	Eighth-eleventh century AD
D	Hindu sculptures Carved panels Architectural fragments
LF	
R	*IAR* 1978-9, 22 Paul 1985, 82-3
N	

31. Sankisa	excavated
L	27°20′05″ N, 79°16′17″ E; 37 km W of Fatehgarh Mound 1 Mound 2, 288 m north of mound 1 Mound 3, 183 m east of mound 2
T	Mound 1: 400 × 300 m, 12 m high Mound 3: 183 × 52 m Rampart: about 3.5 miles in circuit Various structures (Blocks A, B, C, D)
C	PGW cult., NBPW cult., Sunga period, Kushan period, Gupta period

<table>
<tr><td>D</td><td>• Mound 1: present village
• Mound 2:
Brick structure surmounted by a temple; 122 m north of this mound, an Ashoka pillar capital with a standing elephant
• Mound 3:
Brickbats, fragmentary stones
• Rampart:
Earthen duodecagon rampart
• Other small mounds (stupas ?) outside the ramparts:
Sherds: PGW, NBPW, RW
Punch-marked coins, copper coins; Satrap, Indo-Scythian, Indo-Sassanian coins
Terracotta finds: human and animal figurines, moulds, rattle, discs, wheels, beads, bangles, etc.
Stone discs, seals, weights
Miscellaneous objects: bone points and arrow-heads, iron chisels, copper pieces, semi-precious stone beads, ivory pendant and bead
Several inscriptions
Hindu, Buddhist sculptures
Bricks (30 × 20 × 7 cm)
Dwelling deposits (Sunga-Kushan)
Brick wall (Kushan) (maximum brick size: 44 × 27 × 6.5 cm)</td></tr>
<tr><td>LF</td><td></td></tr>
<tr><td>R</td><td>IAR 1955-6, 71
IAR 1995-6, 89-97
Singh 1979, 36
Shrimali 1983, vol. I, 200
Paul 1985, 83-6
Roy 1986, xix
Ghosh 1989, vol. 2, 391-2
Chakrabarti 1997, 191, 251
Chakrabarti et al. 2002, 115</td></tr>
</table>

N	Mound 1, locally called Qilab Mound 2, called Nivi-ka-kot; a monastry according to Cunningham; maybe a *stupa* Mound 2, south of Mound 1 in Singh 1979; in *IAR* 1995-6 Site identified with Sankasya and Sankassa

33. Saurikh	
L	40 km south-east of Fatehgarh Structures west of the village
T	Fort Well
C	Late Historical P.
D	Remains not described
LF	
R	Singh 1979, 106 Paul 1985, 87
N	

34. Surikh	
L	
T	
C	PGW cult., NBPW cult., Early Historical P.
D	Sherds: PGW, NBPW, GW, RW (Early Historical)
LF	
R	*IAR* 1981-2, 110
N	

35. Talgram	
L	Mound S of village
T	Mound
C	Late Historical P.
D	Finds not described
LF	
R	Singh 1979, P. 106
N	Mound called *garhi*

36. Thatia	
L	*Tahsil* Kanauj; 9 km north-east of Jankhat
T	Mound
C	Late Historical P.
D	Finds not described
LF	
R	Singh 1979, 106 Paul 1985, 88
N	Mound occupied until 1858 by a fort

37. Tiuri	
L	27°26′14″ N, 79°20′57″ E
T	Mound: *c.* 1.6 ha, *c.* 5 m high
C	PGW cult.
D	Finds not described
LF	
R	Chakrabarti et al. 2002, 115
N	

KANPUR DISTRICT

213 Site

1. Ahirwah	
L	13 km north-west of Kanpur
T	
C	Late Historical P.
D	Hindu sculptures
LF	
R	Paul 1985, 53
N	Situated on the Grand Trunk Road

2. Ainti	
L	*Tahsil* Ghatampur, 26 km south-west of Ghatampur
T	Fort-mound
C	PGW cult., NBPW cult., Early Historical P.
D	Sherds: PGW, NBPW, RSW Bricks of different sizes
LF	
R	Makkhan Lal 1984, 47 Paul 1985, 53
N	

3. Akbarpur-Birbal	
L	13 km south-west of Ghatampur
T	
C	Early Historical P., Late Historical P.
D	Sherds: NBPW, RSW Hindu sculptures Ancient temple
LF	Sculptures collected in a site called Sita ka Sthana
R	*IAR* 1968-9, 39 Makkhan Lal 1984, 47 Paul 1985, 53
N	

4. Amauli	
L	6 km south of Ghatampur
T	Mounds
C	PGW cult., NBPW cult., Early Historical P.
D	Sherds: BRW, PGW, NBPW, GW, BPW, RSW
LF	
R	*IAR* 1970-1, 39 Makkhan Lal 1984, 47 Paul 1985, 54 Ghosh 1989, vol. 2, 16
N	

5. Amaur or Amour	
L	*Tahsil* Ghatampur, 9 km north-east of Bhitargaon
T	Temple

C	Late Historical P.
D	Brick temple with external decorations of carved bricks
LF	
R	*IAR* 1965-6, 53 Paul 1985, 54
N	Temple known as Mahadeva Baba

6. Ambodha or Amrodha	
L	
T	
C	Late Historical P.
D	Hindu stone sculptures
LF	
R	*IAR* 1980-1, 95 *IAR* 1981-2, 102
N	

7. Amlipur	
L	17 km south of Kanpur
T	
C	Late Historical P.
D	Terracotta figurines Stone sculptures
LF	Collected on a brick platform
R	*IAR* 1970-1, 39 Paul 1985, 54
N	

8. Amsur	
L	12 km from Ghatampur
T	Temple
C	Tenth century AD
D	Carved brick temple with subsequent repairs
LF	
R	Paul 1985, 54
N	

9. Ankin	
L	
T	
C	PGW cult., NBPW cult., Early Historical P.
D	Sherds: PGW, NBPW, RSW
LF	
R	Makkhan Lal 1984, 47
N	

10. Antapur	
L	
T	
C	PGW cult., NBPW cult., Early Historical P.
D	Sherds: PGW, NBPW, RSW
LF	
R	Makkhan Lal 1984, 47
N	

11. Atarra	
L	8 km east of Ghatampur
T	
C	Late Historical P.
D	2 Hindu stone sculptures
LF	Collected in a place known as Narayana Devi
R	Paul 1985, 55
N	

12. Attawa or Attwa	
L	*Tahsil* Gatampur
T	
C	NBPW cult.
D	Sherds
LF	
R	*IAR* 1965-6, 53 Makkhan Lal 1984, 47 Ghosh 1989, vol. 2, 27
N	

13. Atwa	
L	*Tahsil* Kanpur; 8 km east of Bedheuna
T	Mound: 182 × 213 m
C	PGW cult., NBPW cult., Early Historical P.
D	Sherds: PGW, NBPW, RSW, BPW, RW Terracotta heads Hindu sculptures

LF	Sculptures collected in a place known as Bhuiyan Maharani
R	*IAR* 1970-1, 39 Makkhan Lal 1984, 47 Paul 1985, 55
N	

14. Aujhan	
L	
T	
C	PGW cult., NBPW cult., Early Historical P.
D	Sherds: PGW, NBPW, RSW
LF	
R	Makkhan Lal 1984, 47
N	

15. Aunahan	excavated
L	26°37′45″ N, 79°56′45″ E, 60 km west of Kanpur city Mound, west of village
T	Mound: 27 *bighas*, 12 m high
C	Early Historical P., Late Historical P., Sultanate period
D	Sherds: RW (Early Historical P.) Terracotta finds: animal figurines, hopscotchs, wheels, gamesmen, balls, beads etc. Bone arrow-head, pendant Stone engraved object Glass bangles Iron objects Brick structures of re-used Kushan bricks (brick sizes: 33-36 × 20-24 × 5-7 cm, 22 × 18 × 5 cm)

LF	
R	*IAR* 1995-6, 98-103
N	

16. Auron Tahirpur

L	
T	
C	PGW cult.
D	Sherds
LF	
R	Makkhan Lal 1984, 47
N	

17. Bachna

L	
T	
C	NBPW cult., Early Historical P.
D	Sherds: NBPW, RSW
LF	
R	Makkhan Lal 1984, 47
N	

18. Badan-Nivada or Badan-Newada

L	*Tahsil* Bilhaur, near Uttari-Pura
T	Mound Temple

C	NBPW cult., Early Historical P., Eleventh century AD
D	• Mound: Sherds: NBPW, RSW Brickbats • Temple located on a small mound (2-4 m high): Hindu sculptures (eleventh century AD)
LF	
R	Makkhan Lal 1984, 47 Paul 1985, 56
N	Temple known as Muktadevi

19. Badshahpur

L	
T	
C	NBPW cult., Early Historical P.
D	Sherds: NBPW, RSW
LF	
R	Makkhan Lal 1984, 47
N	

20. Bahbalpur

L	
T	
C	NBPW cult., Early Historical P.
D	Sherds: NBPW, RSW
LF	

R	Makkhan Lal 1984, 47
N	

21. Bairi	
L	*Tahsil* Kanpur, on the road Bithur-Kalyanapur
T	Mound: 456 × 322 m, 6 m high
C	NBPW cult., Early Historical P.
D	Sherds: NBPW, BPW, RSW, RW Brickbats
LF	
R	*IAR* 1962-3, 70 Makkhan Lal 1984, 47 Paul 1985, 55 Ghosh 1989, vol. 2, 42
N	

22. Banipara or Banipara Mahraj	
L	26°31′ N, 79°53′ E, *tahsil* Derapur
T	Mound
C	NBPW cult., Early Historical P.
D	Sherds: NBPW, RSW Hindu sculptures (undated)
LF	Sculptures scattered in the village
R	Makkhan Lal 1984, 47 Paul 1985, 56
N	

23. Bara	
L	26°22′ N, 80°01′ E, 37 km west-south-west of Kanpur
T	Mound: 322 m in circuit, 8-10 m high
C	NBPW cult., Early Historical P., Late Historical P.
D	Sherds: NBPW, RSW Copper plate inscription of King Bhoja (AD 836) Medieval sculptures
LF	Sculptures located around the Shiva Temple
R	Makkhan Lal 1984, 47 Paul 1985, 56-7
N	

24. Baraigarhi	
L	26°13′ N, 80°23′ E, 29 km from Kanpur
T	Mound
C	Undated
D	Finds not described
LF	
R	Paul 1985, 57
N	Small fortress in ruins on the mound

25. Barauli	
L	
T	
C	NBPW cult., Early Historical P.
D	Sherds: NBPW, RSW

LF	
R	Makkhan Lal 1984, 47
N	

26. Barhat	
L	3 km south of Bithur
T	Mound: 4-5 m high
C	PGW cult., NBPW cult.; Sultanate, Mughal periods
D	Sherds: PGW, NBPW, BPW, glazed pottery Bricks (45 × 23 × 8 cm, 30 × 18 × 5 cm)
LF	
R	*IAR* 1961-2, 57 Paul 1985, 55 Ghosh 1989, vol. 2, 54
N	

27. Behta	
L	3 km south of Bhitargaon
T	Temple
C	NBPW cult., Early Historical P., Late Historical P.
D	Sherds: NBPW, RSW Hindu sculptures (Gupta, medieval) • Temple: Brick temple of a semicircle shape Numerous architectural members
LF	Some sculptures collected inside the temple

R	*IAR* 1967-8, 47 Makkhan Lal 1984, 47 Paul 1985, 57
N	

28. Benda	
L	6 km west of Ghatampur, on the left side of river Non II
T	Mound
C	Kushan period, Ninth-tenth century AD
D	Hindu stone sculptures
LF	Sculptures collected in a temple on the top of the mound
R	Paul 1985, 57-8
N	

29. Berhat	
L	
T	
C	NBPW cult., Early Historical P.
D	Sherds: NBPW, RSW
LF	
R	Makkhan Lal 1984, 47
N	

30. Bewaine	
L	
T	

C	PGW cult., NBPW cult., Early Historical P.
D	Sherds: PGW, NBPW, RSW
LF	
R	Makkhan Lal 1984, 47
N	

31. Bhadras	
L	6 km NW of Ghatampur
T	Mound: oval perimeter 182 m, 6-8 m high
C	PGW cult., NBPW cult., Early Historical P.
D	Sherds: PGW, NBPW, BPW, GW, RSW, RW
LF	
R	*IAR* 1963-4, 91 Makkhan Lal 1984, 47 Paul 1985, 58 Ghosh 1989, vol. 2, 63
N	Mound known as Devi ka Tila

32. Bhadsa	
L	
T	
C	NBPW cult., Late Historical P.
D	Sherds Sculptures
LF	
R	*IAR* 1964-5, 76 Ghosh 1989, vol. 2, 63
N	

33. Bhaseni	
L	
T	
C	NBPW cult., Early Historical P.
D	Sherds: NBPW, RSW
LF	
R	Makkhan Lal 1984, 47
N	

34. Bherampur	
L	Near Bhimsen Railway Station
T	
C	Tenth century AD
D	Hindu sculptures
LF	Collected on the platform of a modern temple (south of Bherampur)
R	*IAR* 1978-9, 101
N	

35. Bhirhar or Birhar	
L	
T	
C	NBPW cult., Early Historical P., Gupta period
D	Sherds: NBPW, RSW, others (?) Hindu sculptures
LF	Sculptures scattered in the village

R	*IAR* 1967-8, 47 Makkhan Lal 1984, 48 Paul 1985, 60
N	

36. Bhisar	
L	
T	
C	NBPW cult., Early Historical P.
D	Sherds: NBPW, RSW
LF	
R	Makkhan Lal 1984, 47
N	

37. Bhitargaon	
L	26°12′ N, 80°16′ E; 40 km S of Kanpur Mound, 237 m south of temple
T	Temple Mound
C	NBPW cult., Early Historical P., Gupta period
D	Buddhist sculptures (Kushan) • Temple: Brick temple, square in plan, decorated with 120 terracotta panels • Mound: Sherds: NBPW, RSW Sculptures Brickbats
LF	

R	*IAR* 1976-7, 80 Makkhan Lal 1984, 47 Paul 1985, 58 Chakrabarti, Tewari 2000, 115
N	Ancient Phulpur or Flower town (?) Mound: remains of a temple called Jhijhi Naga (?)

38. Bhiwan	
L	
T	
C	NBPW cult., Early Historical P.
D	Sherds: NBPW, RSW
LF	
R	Makkhan Lal 1984, 47
N	

39. Bhul	
L	16 km north-west of Kanpur
T	Mound
C	Undated
D	Finds not described
LF	
R	*IAR* 1970-1, 39 Paul 1985, 60
N	

40. Bihupur	
L	
T	Mound
C	NBPW cult., Ealry Historical P.
D	Sherds: NBPW, BSW, BPW, RSW
LF	
R	*IAR* 1967-8, 46 Makkhan Lal 1984, 47 Ghosh 1989, vol. 2, 76
N	

41. Bijaipur	
L	
T	
C	PGW cult., NBPW cult., Early Historical P.
D	Sherds: BRW, PGW, NBPW, RSW
LF	
R	Makkhan Lal 1984, 48
N	

42. Binaur	
L	26°23′ N, 80°09′ E; 22 km west of Kanpur
T	Mound
C	Early Historical P.
D	Sherds: NBPW, RSW Bricks of different sizes

LF	
R	Makkhan Lal 1984, 48 Paul 1985, 60
N	

43. Birhan	
L	*Tahsil* Derapur; 3 km from Lala Bhagat
T	Mound
C	Undated
D	Finds not described
LF	
R	Paul 1985, 60
N	Sculptures (early medieval) on the mound

44. Biria Derapur	
L	
T	
C	NBPW cult., Early Historical P.
D	Sherds: NBPW, RSW
LF	
R	Makkhan Lal 1984, 48
N	

45. Birohia	
L	
T	

C	Late Historical P.
D	Hindu sculptures
LF	
R	*IAR* 1976-7, 81
N	

46. Birsinghpur	
L	13 km north-east of Ghatampur
T	
C	Ninth-Eleventh century AD
D	Sculptures
LF	Scattered in the village
R	Paul 1985, 60
N	

47. Bithur or Bithoor	
L	26°37′ N, 80°16′ E, 22 km north of Kanpur
T	Mound
C	NBPW cult., Ninth-tenth century AD
D	Copper Hoard Hindu medieval sculptures • Mound: Sherds: NBPW, GW
LF	
R	*IAR* 1955-6, 71 *IAR* 1965-6, 48 *IAR* 1969-70, 41

	Paul 1985, 61 Ghosh 1989, vol. 2, 80
N	Mound known as Valmiki Ashrama Site famous as Brahmavarta Tirtha; identified with Utpalaranya (Dey 1927, 213) or with Pratishtana (other scolars)

48. Blai Khurd	
L	
T	
C	PGW cult., NBPW cult., Early Historical P.
D	Sherds: PGW, NBPW, RSW
LF	
R	Makkan Lal 1984, 47
N	

49. Buhnar	
L	
T	
C	PGW cult., NBPW cult., Early Historical P.
D	Sherds: PGW, NBPW, RSW
LF	
R	Makkhan Lal 1984, 48
N	

50. Chandapur or Chandanpur or Chandnepur	
L	1.5 km south of Musanagar, on the right side of Yamuna
T	Mound
C	PGW cult., NBPW, Early Historical P., Late Historical P.
D	Sherds: PGW, NBPW, RSW Terracotta figurines (Kushan) Carved capital of a *torana* in red sandstone (Kushan) Hindu sculptures (Kushan, medieval) Decorated architectural members (Kushan)
LF	
R	*IAR* 1968-9, 39 *IAR* 1976-7, 53, 81 *IAR* 1977-8, 84 *IAR* 1980-1, 95 Makkhan Lal 1984, 48 Paul 1985, 62 Ghosh 1989, vol. 2, 93
N	In Makkhan Lal there is another Chandanpur without PGW

51. Chanwar	
L	9 km north-west of Ghatampur
T	Mound Temple *Stupa*
C	NBPW cult., Sunga-Kushan period, Late Historical P.
D	• Mound: Sherds: NBPW, GW, BSW, RW (Sunga-Kushan) Terracotta figurines (Gupta) Tribal coin Sculptures

	Bricks (55 × 57 × 7 cm, 50 × 26 × 7 cm), brickbats • Temple: Remains of a carved brick temple, square in plan (ninth-tenth century) • *Stupa* in ruins
LF	Sculptures collected at the top of the mound (modern temple) and close to the brick temple
R	*IAR* 1980-1, 71 *IAR* 1981-2, 102 *IAR* 1985-6, 171 Paul 1985, 61-2
N	

52. Chaparehata or Chaparghata or Chaprehata or Chaparghat	
L	*Tahsil* Bhoganipur, 3 km west of Musanagar
T	Mound
C	Early Historical P., Late Historical P.
D	Sherds: NBPW, RSW, BRW, BSW, RW Terracotta figurines Stone sculptures (ninth-eleventh century AD) Remains of a decorated parapet Architectural members Brickbats
LF	
R	*IAR* 1968-9, 39 *IAR* 1992-3, 94 Makkhan Lal 1984, 48 Paul 1985, 62
N	Indo-Islamic fort close to the mound

53. Chaurah	
L	
T	
C	Early Historical P.
D	Sherds: NBPW, RSW
LF	
R	Makkhan Lal 1984, 48
N	

54. Chhatarpur	
L	18 km SE of Bilhaur
T	Temples (three)
C	Late Historical P.
D	Copper plate inscription (AD 1120) • Temple 1: Carved panel Few stone carved pieces • Temple 2: Hindu sculptures (medieval) Several ornamental architectural members • Temple 3: Hindu stone sculptures (eighth-ninth century) Buddha head (fifth-sixth century) Carved architectural members (eighth-ninth century)
LF	
R	Paul 1985, 62-3
N	Village surrounded with a brick wall

55. Chhatereva	
L	
T	
C	Late Historical P.
D	Sculptures
LF	
R	*IAR* 1970-1, 69
N	

56. Chilauli	
L	
T	
C	Early Historical P.
D	Sherds: NBPW, RSW
LF	
R	Makkhan Lal 1984, 48
N	

57. Debipur	
L	
T	
C	PGW cult., NBPW cult., Early Historical P.
D	Sherds: GW, NBPW, RSW
LF	
R	Makkhan Lal 1984, 48
N	

58. Deoha	
L	
T	
C	NBPW cult., Early Historical P.
D	Sherds: NBPW, RSW
LF	
R	Makkhan Lal 1984, 48
N	

59. Digh	
L	Near the confluence Yamuna–Sengar
T	
C	Late Historical P.
D	Hindu sculptures
LF	
R	*IAR* 1968-9, 39
N	

60. Dul	
L	17 km north-west of Kanpur
T	Mound
C	Undated
D	Finds not described
LF	
R	Paul 1985, 63
N	

61. Durgapur	
L	
T	
C	Early Historical P.
D	Sherds: NBPW, RSW
LF	
R	Makkhan Lal 1984, 48
N	

62. Fattepur	
L	
T	
C	First-second century AD
D	Stone sculptures Structural members
LF	
R	*IAR* 1992-3, 94
N	

63. Gadankhera	
L	23 km west of Kanpur
T	Mound
C	Undated
D	Sherds Brickbats and carved bricks Traces of an ancient temple

LF	
R	Paul 1985, 65
N	

64. Gaganpura Charsa	
L	
T	
C	Early Historical P.
D	Sherds: NBPW, RSW
LF	
R	Makkhan Lal 1984, 48
N	

65. Gahlon	
L	
T	
C	NBPW cult., Early Historical P.
D	Sherds: NBPW, RSW
LF	
R	Makkhan Lal 1984, 48
N	

66. Galatha	
L	
T	
C	PGW cult., NBPW cult., Early Historical P.

D	Sherds: BRW, PGW, NBPW, RSW
LF	
R	Makkhan Lal 1984, 48
N	

67. Garhia Sikandra	
L	
T	
C	Early Historical P.
D	Sherds: NBPW, RSW
LF	
R	Makkhan Lal 1984, 48
N	

68. Gaupur	
L	
T	
C	Early Historical P.
D	Sherds: NBPW, RSW
LF	
R	Makkhan Lal 1984, 48
N	

69. Ghatampur	
L	26°9′ N, 80°10′ E Temple, 1 km south of town

T	Temple
C	Eleventh-twelfth century AD, Eighteenth century AD
D	Fragmentary Hindu sculptures Mughal inscription (AD 1703-4) Brick temple in ruins
LF	
R	*IAR* 1977-8, 71 Paul 1985, 65
N	Site traditionally founded by Ghatam Deo

70. Ghatwa	
L	
T	
C	NBPW cult., Early Historical P.
D	Sherds: NBPW, RSW
LF	
R	Makkhan Lal 1984, 48
N	

71. Gilwat	
L	
T	
C	NBPW cult., Early Historical P.
D	Sherds: NBPW, RSW
LF	
R	Makkhan Lal 1984, 48
N	

72. Gobalpur	
L	
T	
C	Early Historical P.
D	Sherds: NBPW, RSW
LF	
R	Makkhan Lal 1984, 48
N	

73. Gobrauri	
L	
T	
C	NBPW cult., Early Historical P.
D	Sherds: NBPW, RSW
LF	
R	Makkhan Lal 1984, 48
N	

74. Goraya	
L	
T	
C	NBPW cult., Early Historical P.
D	Sherds: NBPW, RSW
LF	
R	Makkhan Lal 1984, 48
N	

75. Gurdahi Khurd	
L	
T	
C	Early Historical P.
D	Sherds: NBPW, RSW
LF	
R	Makkhan Lal 1984, 48
N	

76. Gurgawan	
L	
T	
C	NBPW cult., Early Historical P.
D	Sherds: NBPW, RSW
LF	
R	Makkhan Lal 1984, 48
N	

77. Halia	
L	*Tahsil* Bhoganipur
T	
C	NBPW cult., Late Historical P.
D	Sherds: BRW, NBPW, RW Medieval sculptures
LF	
R	*IAR* 1992-3, 94
N	

78. Halpura	
L	11 km north-west of Bilhaur
T	
C	Ninth-Eleventh century AD
D	Sculptures
LF	Scattered in the village
R	Paul 1985, 65
N	

79. Harha	
L	24 km south-west of Kanpur
T	
C	Ninth-tenth century AD
D	Stone sculptures
LF	
R	Paul 1985, 65
N	

80. Hathei	
L	
T	
C	NBPW cult., Early Historical P.
D	Sherds: NBPW, RSW
LF	
R	Makkhan Lal 1984, 48
N	

81. Hathigawan	
L	
T	
C	NBPW cult., Early Historical P.
D	Sherds: NBPW, RSW
LF	
R	Makkhan Lal 1984, 48
N	

82. Hathipur	
L	12 km south-east of Kanpur
T	Mound
C	Late Historical P., Twelfth-Thirteenth century AD
D	Sherds Hindu sculptures Architectural members
LF	
R	Paul 1985, 66
N	

83. Hingurpur–Pingupur	
L	3 km SW of Bithur, on the bank of river Non I
T	Mound
C	Undated
D	Sherds Brickbats

LF	
R	Paul 1985, 66
N	

84. Hulasipur	
L	
T	
C	Early Historical P.
D	Sherds: NBPW, RSW
LF	
R	Makkhan Lal 1984, 48
N	

85. Indayan	
L	
T	
C	PGW cult., NBPW cult., Early Historical P.
D	Sherds: BRW, PGW, NBPW, RSW
LF	
R	Makkhan Lal 1984, 48
N	

86. Indira Nagar	
L	Mound, 1 km north of Kalyanpur (railway station)
T	Mound: 200 × 200 m, 6 m high
C	OCP cult.

D	Sherds: OCP, BSW, BRW, RW, GW Pre-harappan terracotta seal
LF	
R	Shukla 1987, 55-8
N	

87. Indrukh	
L	
T	
C	NBPW cult., Early Historical P.
D	Sherds: NBPW, RSW
LF	
R	Makkhan Lal 1984, 48
N	

88. Jahangirabad or Jhangirabad	
L	26°11′ N, 80°10′ E, 5.5 km north-east of Ghatampur
T	Mound: *c.* 10 acres, 5 m high
C	Sixth century BC, PGW cult., NBPW cult., Early Historical P.
D	Sherds: PGW, BRW, NBPW, GW, BPW, RSW, RW
LF	
R	*IAR* 1965-6, 53 *IAR* 1967-8, 46 *IAR* 1968-9, 39 *BMA* 40, 62 Tripathi 1976, 126

	Makkhan Lal 1984, 48 Paul 1985, 66 Ghosh 1989, vol. 2, 179, 185 Chakrabarti, Tewari 2000, 115
N	

89. Jaimou	
L	
T	
C	Late Historical P.
D	Hindu sculptures
LF	Devi's Temple
R	*IAR* 1971-2, 79-80
N	

90. Jajmau	excavated
L	26°28′ N, 80°21′ E 5 km east of Kanpur
T	Mound: 1-2 km × 200 m, 20-30 m high
C	PGW cult., NBPW cult., Early Historic P., Late Historic P.
D	Sherds: BRW, PGW, NBPW, BPW, GW, RSW, RW Tribal coin, punch-marked coins Seals with *brahmi* inscriptions Buddhist seal (Gupta) Terracotta finds: human and animal figurines, *dampati* plaques, discs, lids, beads, smoothers, dabbers, seals Bone and ivory bracelets Agate and carnelian beads

	Hivory seals with *brahmi* script (third century BC, early century AD) Inscribed stone tablet Iron objects: arrow-heads, rings, nails, etc. Damaged sculpture in red sandstone (Gupta) Bricks: 38-39 × 24-25 × 4-5 cm (Kushan), 48 × 24 × 7 cm Walls of re-used bricks, brickbats Remains of structural activity
LF	
R	*IAR* 1956-7, 29 *IAR* 1957-8, 49 *IAR* 1961-2, 57, 91-93 *IAR* 1968-9, 39, 52 *IAR* 1973-4, 31 *IAR* 1974-5, 48 *IAR* 1975-6, 52-53 *IAR* 1976-7, 54 BMA 40, 62 Tripathi 1976, 126 Makkhan Lal 1984, 48 Paul 1985, 66-8 Possehl 1986, 44-5 Ghosh 1989, vol. 2, 180
N	Known also as Bazidpur; in ancient times as Siddhapuri, Siddhipur, Yayatipur

91. Jeora	
L	3 km north-west of Kanpur
T	Mound: 1 km in length, 10-12 m high
C	PGW cult., NBPW cult., Tenth-eleventh century AD
D	Sherds: PGW, NBPW, BPW, RW Cubical terracotta tablet with three incised lines Few stone sculptures (tenth-eleventh century AD)

LF	Sculptures collected in a temple on the top of the mound
R	Paul 1985, 68
N	

92. Kakwan	
L	
T	
C	Early Historical P.
D	Sherds: NBPW, RSW
LF	
R	Makkhan Lal 1984, 48
N	

93. Kalyanpur	
L	26°29′ N, 80°15′ E, 9 km NW of Kanpur
T	
C	Early Medieval P.
D	Hindu stone sculptures Architectural carved members
LF	Sculptures collected in Somanatha Temple
R	*IAR* 1969-70, 41 *IAR* 1970-1, 39 Paul 1985, 69
N	

94. Kamalpur	
L	
T	
C	Early Historical P.
D	Sherds: NBPW, RSW
LF	
R	Makkhan Lal 1984, 48
N	

95. Kamasia	
L	
T	
C	PGW cult., NBPW cult., Early Historical P.
D	Sherds: PGW, NBPW, RSW
LF	
R	Makkhan Lal 1984, 48
N	

96. Kamsan	
L	
T	
C	NBPW cult., Early Historical P.
D	Sherds: NBPW, RSW
LF	
R	Makkhan Lal 1984, 48
N	

97. Karankhara	
L	
T	
C	PGW cult., NBPW cult.
D	Sherds: PGW, NBPW
LF	
R	Makkhan Lal 1984, 49
N	

98. Karchalipur	
L	20 km east of Ghatampur
T	Mound
C	PGW cult., NBPW cult., Early Historical P., Late Historical P.
D	Sherds: PGW, NBPW, BPW, BSW, GW, BRW Stone sculptures Architectural members
LF	Sculptures and architectural members re-used in the structure of Aleshvara Mahadeva temple
R	*IAR* 1967-8, 47 *IAR* 1968-9, 39 Makkhan Lal 1984, 49 Paul 1985, 75 Ghosh 1989, vol. 2, 206
N	In Makkhan Lal there is another Karchalipur without PGW

99. Kashipur	
L	
T	Three sites
C	PGW cult., NBPW cult., Early Historical P.
D	• Site A: Sherds: PGW, NBPW, RSW • Site B: Sherds: NBPW, RSW • Site C: Sherds: NBPW, RSW
LF	
R	Makkhan Lal 1984, 49
N	

100. Katar	
L	*Tahsil* Ghatampur, 3 km south of Musanagar Mound 1, the village Mound 2, 2 km south of village
T	Mounds (two) Platforms
C	Sunga period, Kushan period, Late Historical P.
D	• Mound 1: Sherds (Kushan, Gupta) Brickbats • Mound 2: Monolithic pillar in red stone (Sunga) Stone architectural member with *brahmi* inscription (first century BC) 6 carved architectural members with Buddhist subjects • Platforms: Sculptures (fifth-seventh century AD)

LF	
R	*IAR* 1992-3, 95 Paul 1990 Chakrabarti, Tewari 2000, 115
N	Platforms locally called Shankar Baba Chabutara or Athai Chabutara Mound 2 known as Devaliya Daddha Baba; probably a Sunga *stupa*

101. Katka	
L	
T	
C	PGW cult., NBPW cult., Early Historical P.
D	Sherds: PGW, NBPW, RSW
LF	
R	Makkhan Lal 1984, 49
N	

102. Keilai	
L	
T	
C	NBPW cult., Early Historical P.
D	Sherds: NBPW, RSW
LF	
R	Makkhan Lal 1984, 49
N	

103. Keshwa	
L	*Tahsil* Bhoganipur
T	
C	Late Historical P.
D	Sculptures
LF	
R	*IAR* 1992-3, 94
N	

104. Khajuri	
L	
T	
C	NBPW cult., Early Historical P.
D	Sherds: NBPW, RSW
LF	
R	Makkhan Lal 1984, 49
N	

105. Khalla	
L	
T	
C	Early Historical P.
D	Sherds: NBPW, RSW
LF	
R	Makkhan Lal 1984, 49
N	

106. Kheera	
L	
T	
C	PGW cult., NBPW cult.
D	Sherds: PGW, NBPW, GW, RW
LF	
R	*IAR* 1975-6, 8
N	

107. Kheora	
L	On the right bank of the Ganges
T	
C	PGW cult., NBPW cult., Sultanate, Mughal periods
D	Sherds: PGW, NBPW, BRW, RSW, RW, glazed pottery Copper coin
LF	
R	*IAR* 1976-7, 53 Makkhan Lal 1984, 49
N	

108. Khera	
L	*Tahsil* Ghatampur
T	
C	Late Historical P.
D	Hindu sculptures
LF	Scattered in the village

R	*IAR* 1967-8, 47
N	

109. Kherakursi	
L	
T	
C	PGW cult., NBPW cult., Early Historical P.
D	Sherds: PGW, NBPW, RSW
LF	
R	Makkhan Lal 1984, 49
N	

110. Khirianpurva or Khirian Purwa	
L	*Tahsil* Bhoganipur
T	
C	Undated
D	Terracotta figurines Sculptures
LF	
R	*IAR* 1992-3, 94
N	

111. Khirsa	
L	*Tahsil* Kanpur
T	Mound
C	Early Historical P.

D	Sherds: NBPW, RSW
LF	
R	*IAR* 1970-1, 39 Makkhan Lal 1984, 49
N	

112. Kisankhera	
L	
T	
C	NBPW cult., Early Historical P.
D	Sherds: NBPW, RSW
LF	
R	Makkhan Lal 1984, 49
N	

113. Kishora	
L	
T	
C	Early Historical P.
D	Sherds: NBPW, RSW
LF	
R	Makkhan Lal 1984, 49
N	

114. Kismara	
L	
T	
C	Early Historical P.
D	Sherds: NBPW, RSW
LF	
R	Makkhan Lal 1984, 49
N	

115. Kumbhi	
L	6 km south-west of Akbarpur, on the bank of river Sengar
T	Mound
C	Late Historical P.
D	Hindu stone sculptures
LF	
R	*IAR* 1980-1, 95 *IAR* 1981-2, 102 Paul 1985, 75
N	Mound known as Lakarpur

116. Kurain	
L	26°05′ N, 80°13′ E, 12 km south-east of Ghatampur
T	Mound: 5-6 m high Temple
C	NBPW cult., Early Historical P., Ninth-tenth century AD, Fourteenth-fifteenth century AD

D	• Mound: Sherds: NBPW, BPW, BSW, RSW, RW Terracotta female figurine Hindu sculptures (ninth-tenth century AD) Architectural members • Temple in bricks (fourteenth-fifteenth century AD)
LF	Sculptures and architectural members scattered in the village
R	*IAR* 1969-70, 41 *IAR* 1970-1, 39 Makkhan Lal 1984, 49 Paul 1985, 75 Ghosh 1989, vol. 2, 245
N	Temple locally known as Mahadeva Baba

117. Kursenda	
L	6 km south-west of Ghatampur
T	Mound: 60 m^2, 3-4 m high
C	Late Historical P.
D	Sherds Hindu stone sculptures
LF	
R	*IAR* 1967-8, 47 Paul 1985, 75-6
N	

118. Kurtha	
L	5 km east of Bhitargaon
T	Temple
C	Early Historical P., Tenth century AD

D	Sherds: NBPW, RSW Ruined brick temple
LF	
R	Makkhan Lal 1984, 49 Paul 1985, 76
N	

119. Lakhan	
L	*Tahsil* Ghatampur
T	
C	Late Historical P.
D	Sculptures
LF	Scattered in the village
R	*IAR* 1967-8, 47
N	

120. Lalabhagat or Lal Bhagat	
L	26°44′ N, 79°51′ E; 26 km south-west of Bilhaur
T	Mound
C	Early Historical P.
D	Sherds: NBPW, RSW, RW Terracotta female figurine Cooper coin (Kshatrapa) Red sandstone carved pillar (Kushan) with fragmentary *brahmi* inscription Bricks (45 × 25 × 3.5 cm)
LF	Pillar located on the top of the mound

R	*IAR* 1970-1, 69 Makkhan Lal 1984, 49 Paul 1985, 76-7 Ghosh 1989, vol. 2, 250
N	

121. Lalpur	
L	*Tahsil* Ghatampur
T	
C	NBPW cult.
D	Sherds
LF	
R	*IAR* 1965-6, 53 Ghosh 1989, vol. 2, 251
N	

122. Lamahra	
L	
T	
C	PGW cult., NBPW cult., Early Historical P.
D	Sherds: PGW, NBPW, RSW
LF	
R	Makkhan Lal 1984, 49
N	

123. Machaila	
L	*Tahsil* Ghatampur
T	
C	Undated
D	Polished stone celt
LF	
R	*IAR* 1992-3, 95
N	

124. Madar Rai	
L	
T	
C	Late Historical P.
D	Hindu sculptures Architectural members
LF	
R	*IAR* 1976-7, 81
N	

125. Magarsa or Magrasa	
L	15 km south-west of Kanpur
T	Mounds (two)
C	Late Historical P.
D	• Mound 1: Remains of old (?) fort • Mound 2: Hindu sculptures Pedestals with inscription in *nagari* characters

LF	
R	*IAR* 1964-5, 76 Paul 1985, 77
N	

126. Mahraipur	
L	
T	
C	NBPW cult., Early Historical P.
D	Sherds: NBPW, RSW
LF	
R	Makkhan Lal 1984, 49
N	

127. Mahrajnagar	
L	
T	
C	Early Historical P.
D	Sherds: NBPW, RSW
LF	
R	Makkhan Lal 1984, 49
N	

128. Mahulia	
L	
T	

C	NBPW cult., Early Historical P.
D	Sherds: NBPW, RSW
LF	
R	Makkhan Lal 1984, 49
N	

129. Makanpur	
L	13 km north-west of Bilhaur
T	
C	Tenth-eleventh century AD
D	Sherds Hindu, Jaina stone sculptures Carved architectural members
LF	Sculptures collected in Kherapati temple
R	*IAR* 1976-7, 81 *IAR* 1982-3, 139 Paul 1985, 77
N	

130. Mandauli	
L	
T	
C	NBPW cult., Early Historical P.
D	Sherds: NBPW, RSW
LF	
R	Makkhan Lal 1984, 49
N	

131. Maraha	
L	9 km west of Jankhat
T	
C	Gupta period
D	Sculptures
LF	
R	Paul 1985, 77
N	

132. Matai Kisanpur or Mati Kisanpur	
L	8 km south-west of Bara
T	Mound
C	NBPW cult.
D	Sherds
LF	
R	*IAR* 1955-6, 71 Makkhan Lal 1984, 49 Paul 1985, 78 Ghosh 1989, vol. 2, 286
N	

133. Math of Pisnarin	
L	
T	
C	Tenth century AD
D	Bricks

LF	
R	*BMA* 40, 62
N	

134. Mathurapur	
L	
T	
C	Early Historical P.
D	Sherds: NBPW, RSW
LF	
R	Makkhan Lal 1984, 49
N	

135. Mau	
L	
T	
C	NBPW cult.
D	Sherds
LF	
R	*IAR* 1976-7, 53
N	

136. Mawar	
L	
T	
C	PGW cult., NBPW cult., Early Historical P.

D	Sherds: PGW, NBPW, RSW
LF	
R	Makkhan Lal 1984, 49
N	

137. Milanpur	
L	
T	
C	PGW cult., NBPW cult., Early Historical P.
D	Sherds: PGW, NBPW, RSW
LF	
R	Makkhan Lal 1984, 49
N	

138. Musanagar	excavated
L	26°10′ N, 79°50′ E or 26°09′ N, 79°57′ E; *tahsil* Bhognipur
T	Mound
C	PGW cult., NBPW cult., Early Historical P., Late Historical P., Eighteenth century AD
D	Sherds: PGW, NBPW, BRW, BSW, GW, RSW, RW (Sunga-Kushan), others (?) Smooth stone axe Terracotta finds: seals, figurines (Sunga), sling-balls, discs, bangles, inscribed tablet (first century BC) Bone points, arrow-heads Copper antimony rods Few iron implements Sculptures (Sunga-Kushan, Gupta, Eighth-tenth century AD) Fragments of parapet pillars (Sunga)

	Inscribed bricks and bowl in *brahmi* characters Mughal inscription (1745) Roof-tiles Carved architectural members Traces of dwellings (wattle-and-daub) Brich structures (brick size: 34 × 26 × 8 cm)
LF	Sculptures collected in the Muktadevi temple Museum Inscribed tablet preserved in the Bharat Kala Bhavan (Varanasi)
R	*IAR* 1955-6, 69 *IAR* 1967-8, 47 *IAR* 1977-8, 71 *IAR* 1980-1, 71 *IAR* 1992-3, 93 *IAR* 1994-5, 74-6 *IAR* 1995-6, 103-4 *BMA* 40, 62 Tripathi 1976, 128 Makkhan Lal 1984, 49 Paul 1985, 78 Chakrabarti, Tewari 2000, 115
N	Pillars connected with a Buddhist *stupa* (first century BC)

139. Nabiya-Khera	
L	
T	Temple
C	Tenth century AD
D	Brick temple in ruins
LF	
R	*IAR* 1960-1, 67
N	

140. Narainpur	
L	
T	
C	Early Historical P.
D	Sherds: NBPW, RSW
LF	
R	Makkhan Lal 1984, 49
N	

141. Nariha	
L	
T	
C	NBPW cult., Maurya period, Sunga-Kushan period
D	Sherds: NBPW, RSW, RW Terracottas (Sunga-Kushan) Hindu stone sculptures Bricks (Sunga, Maurya) Architectural members
LF	
R	*IAR* 1981-2, 102
N	

142. Narkhurd	
L	
T	
C	Early Historical P.
D	Sherds: NBPW, RSW

LF	
R	Makkhan Lal 1984, 49
N	

143. Narwal

L	26°14′ N, 80°26′ E; 29 km south of Kanpur
T	
C	Late Historical P.
D	Terracotta head Hindu sculptures Fragmentary architectural members
LF	Terracotta head preserved in the National Museum New Delhi
R	*IAR* 1980-1, 95 *IAR* 1981-2, 102 Paul 1985, 78
N	

144. Naubasta

L	*Tahsil* Kanpur
T	
C	Late Historical P.
D	Sculptures
LF	
R	*IAR* 1970-1, 39
N	

145. Naurangabad	
L	*Tahsil* Kanpur
T	
C	Late Historical P.
D	Sculptures
LF	
R	*IAR* 1970-1, 39
N	

146. Nawabganj	
L	Kanpur suburbs, left side of river Ganga
T	Mound
C	PGW cult., NBPW cult., Sunga-Kushan period
D	Sherds: PGW, NBPW, BRW, RSW, Sunga-Kushan pottery
LF	
R	*IAR* 1977-8, 57 Makkhan Lal 1984, 49
N	

147. Nayapurwa	
L	On the left side of the Yamuna
T	
C	Undated
D	Sherds: BRW, BSW, GW, RW Terracotta figurines
LF	

R	*IAR* 1992-3, 94
N	

148. Nemaniakhera or Nebiyakhera or Nibiya Khera	
L	12 km south-east of Ghatampur
T	Temple Mound (several mounds in Ghosh 1989)
C	NBPW cult., Early Historical P., Late Historical P.
D	Sculptures (Gupta, medieval) • Temple: Ruined octagonal brick temple with sculptures • Mound: Sherds: NBPW, RSW, RW Terracotta female head
LF	
R	*IAR* 1969-70, 41 *IAR* 1970-1, 39 Makkhan Lal 1984, 49 Paul 1985, 79 Ghosh 1989, vol. 2, 317
N	

149. Nihura	
L	
T	
C	Late Historical P.
D	Hindu sculptures
LF	

R	*IAR* 1968-9, 39
N	

150. Nonha Narsingh

L	
T	
C	PGW cult., NBPW cult., Early Historical P.
D	Sherds: BRW, PGW, NBPW, RSW
LF	
R	Makkhan Lal 1984, 49
N	

151. Ozham

L	
T	
C	PGW cult., NBPW cult.
D	Sherds
LF	
R	*IAR* 1970-1, 69 Tripathi 1976, 129 Ghosh 1989, vol. 2, 322
N	

152. Padri-Lalpur or Lalpur

L	26°13′ N, 80°14′ E, 5 km north-west of Bhitargaon
T	Mound: 215 m^2, 6-7 m high

C	NBPW cult., Early Historical P.
D	Sherds: NBPW, BSW, BPW, RSW, GW, RW
LF	
R	*IAR* 1967-8, 46 Makkhan Lal 1984, 49 Paul 1985, 79 Ghosh 1989, vol. 2, 324
N	

153. Pahewa	
L	9 km E of Ghatampur
T	
C	Early Historical P., Late Historical P.
D	Sherds: NBPW, RSW Hindu sculptures
LF	
R	*IAR* 1967-8, 47 Makkhan Lal 1984, 49 Paul 1985, 79
N	

154. Palahpur	
L	
T	
C	PGW cult., NBPW cult., Early Historical P.
D	Sherds: PGW, NBPW, RSW
LF	
R	Makkhan Lal 1984, 49
N	

155. Panchgawan	
L	
T	
C	PGW cult., NBPW cult., Early Historical P.
D	Sherds: BRW, PGW, NBPW, RSW
LF	
R	Makkhan Lal 1984, 49
N	

156. Panka	
L	
T	
C	Early Historical P.
D	Sherds: NBPW, RSW
LF	
R	Makkhan Lal 1984, 49
N	

157. Panki	
L	
T	
C	Early Historical P.
D	Sherds: NBPW, RSW
LF	
R	Makkhan Lal 1984, 49
N	

158. Pankiganga	
L	*Tahsil* Kanpur
T	Mound
C	Undated
D	Finds not described
LF	
R	*IAR* 1970-1, 39
N	

159. Paras	
L	8 km south-east of Ghatampur
T	
C	Early Medieval P.
D	Stone sculptures
LF	
R	*IAR* 1967-8, 46 Paul 1985, 81
N	

160. Parauli	
L	4 km north of Bhitargaon
T	Temple
C	Tenth-eleventh century AD
D	Ruined brick temple: bricks with deep reliefs
LF	
R	Paul 1985, 81
N	

161. Parsaurah	
L	
T	
C	Early Historical P.
D	Sherds: NBPW, RSW
LF	
R	Makkhan Lal 1984, 49
N	

162. Pasikhera	
L	
T	
C	NBPW, Early Historical P.
D	Sherds: NBPW, RSW
LF	
R	Makkhan Lal 1984, 50
N	

163. Pichora	
L	
T	
C	Early Historical P.
D	Sherds: NBPW, RSW
LF	
R	Makkhan Lal 1984, 50
N	

164. Pipergaon or Pepergawan	
L	*Tahsil* Kanpur
T	
C	Early Historical P., Late Historical P.
D	Sherds: NBPW, RSW Sculptures
LF	
R	*IAR* 1970-1, 39 Makkhan Lal 1984, 50
N	

165. Pooran Purwa	
L	
T	
C	NBPW cult., Early Historical P.
D	Sherds: NBPW, RSW
LF	
R	Makkhan Lal 1984, 50
N	

166. Pratappur	
L	
T	
C	NBPW cult.
D	Sherds: NBPW, BSW, RW Polished stone axe (undated)

LF	
R	*IAR* 1992-3, 94
N	

167. Pura Sukul	
L	
T	
C	NBPW cult., Early Historical P.
D	Sherds: NBPW, RSW
LF	
R	Makkhan Lal 1984, 50
N	

168. Radhan	
L	*Tahsil* Bilhaur, 4 km north-east of Uttaripura
T	Mound
C	PGW cult., NBPW cult., Gupta period, Eighth-tenth century AD
D	Sherds: PGW, BRW, NBPW, BPW, RSW, RW Few stone sculptures
LF	Sculptures housed in a modern temple (east of mound)
R	*IAR* 1976-7, 53, 81 *IAR* 1986-7, 131 Makkhan Lal 1984, 50 Paul 1985, 81
N	C^{14} dates in *IAR* 1986-7

169. Rahiniyapur	
L	
T	
C	NBPW cult., Early Historical P., Late Historical P.
D	Sherds: NBPW, others (?) Hindu sculptures
LF	
R	*IAR* 1980-1, 71, 95
N	

170. Rahmpur Bisdhan	
L	
T	
C	PGW cult., NBPW cult., Early Historical P.
D	Sherds: PGW, NBPW, RSW
LF	
R	Makkhan Lal 1984, 50
N	

171. Rahnas	
L	10 km north-east of Narwal
T	Fort Temple
C	Late Historical P.
D	• Temple (ruined): Few Hindu stone sculptures Two inscribed stone-slabs in *devanagari* characters (thirteenth century AD) • Fort in ruins

LF	
R	*IAR* 1967-8, 46 *IAR* 1970-1, 55 Paul 1985, 82
N	Site mentioned in the inscription as Rahanatha Ruined temple site called Lathiyre-Baba

172. Raipur

L	
T	
C	NBPW cult., Early Historical P.
D	Sherds: NBPW, RSW
LF	
R	Makkhan Lal 1984, 50
N	

173. Ramaipura or Ramaipur

L	*Tahsil* Kanpur
T	Mound
C	Late Historical P.
D	Sherds
LF	
R	*IAR* 1970-1, 39 *IAR* 1980-1, 95 *IAR* 1981-2, 102
N	

174. Ramel	
L	2 km south of Bithur, on the left bank of river Non
T	
C	Eighth-tenth century AD
D	Few sculptures
LF	
R	Paul 1985, 82
N	

175. Ramsari	
L	
T	Mound
C	Late Historical P.
D	Sherds
LF	
R	*IAR* 1985-6, 116
N	

176. Ranipur	
L	
T	
C	NBPW cult., Early Historical P.
D	Sherds: NBPW, RSW
LF	
R	Makkhan Lal 1984, 50
N	

177. Rar	
L	16 km south of Bhitargaon
T	Temple
C	Tenth-eleventh century AD (?)
D	Brick temple decorated as Parauli temple
LF	
R	Paul 1985, 82
N	

178. Rasdhan	
L	13 km from Akbarpur
T	Mound
C	NBPW cult., Early Historical P., Eighth-eleventh century AD
D	Sherds: NBPW, RSW Hindu sculptures Brickbats Carved architectural members Remains of a fort surrounded by dich
LF	Architectural members located in the Durgadevi Temple
R	*IAR* 1976-7, 53, 81 Makkhan Lal 1984, 50 Paul 1985, 82
N	

179. Rasulpur Bhuranda	
L	
T	

C	PGW cult., NBPW cult., Early Historical P.
D	Sherds: PGW, NBPW, RSW
LF	
R	Makkhan Lal 1984, 50
N	

180. Rataipur	
L	*Tahsil* Ghatampur
T	Mounds
C	NBPW cult., Early Historical P.
D	Sherds: NBPW, RSW
LF	
R	*IAR* 1970-1, 39 Makkhan Lal 1984, 50 Ghosh 1989, vol. 2, 373
N	

181. Ratanpur	
L	
T	
C	PGW cult., NBPW cult., Early Historical P.
D	Sherds: PGW, NBPW, RSW
LF	
R	Makkhan Lal 1984, 50
N	

182. Reona	
L	
T	
C	NBPW cult., Early Historical P.
D	Sherds: NBPW, RSW
LF	
R	*IAR* 1968-9, 39 Makkhan Lal 1984, 50 Ghosh 1989, vol. 2, 375
N	

183. Rihiniyapur	
L	
T	Mound
C	NBPW cult., Early Historical P., Late Historical P.
D	Hindu sculptures Architectural fragmets • Mound: Sherds: NBPW, BPW (Early Historical P.), RW (medieval)
LF	
R	*IAR* 1981-2, 102
N	Mound locally called Khareswara or Kanshasan

184. Rohini	
L	
T	
C	NBPW cult., Early Historical P.

D	Sherds: NBPW, RSW
LF	
R	*IAR* 1976-7, 53 Makkhan Lal 1984, 50
N	

185. Salempur Mahera

L	
T	
C	Early Historical P.
D	Sherds: NBPW, RSW
LF	
R	Makkhan Lal 1984, 50
N	

186. Sambhalgarh

L	
T	
C	PGW cult., NBPW cult., Early Historical P.
D	Sherds: PGW, NBPW
LF	
R	Makkhan Lal 1984, 50
N	

187. Sambhua or Sambhuwa	
L	8 km west of Bhitargaon
T	Temple Fields close the temple
C	Early Historical P., Late Historical P.
D	Sherds: BPW, RSW Sculptures Plastered brick temple
LF	
R	*IAR* 1970-1, 69 Makkhan Lal 1984, 50 Paul 1985, 83
N	

188. Sandila	
L	
T	
C	NBPW cult., Early Historical P.
D	Sherds: NBPW, RSW
LF	
R	Makkhan Lal 1984, 50
N	

189. Sanihapur	
L	
T	
C	PGW cult., NBPW cult., Early Historical P.

D	Sherds: PGW, NBPW, RSW
LF	
R	Makkhan Lal 1984, 50
N	

190. Sanjeti Badshahpur	
L	
T	
C	PGW cult., NBPW cult., Early Historical P.
D	Sherds: PGW, NBPW, RSW
LF	
R	Makkhan Lal 1984, 50
N	

191. Sankhin Buzurg or Sankim Buzurg	
L	
T	
C	NBPW cult., Early Historical P.
D	Sherds: NBPW, RSW
LF	
R	*IAR* 1976-7, 53 Makkhan Lal 1984, 50
N	

192. Sanon	
L	*Tahsil* Kanpur, 3 km south-east of Sachandi
T	Mound
C	NBPW cult., Early Historical P.
D	Sherds: NBPW, BPW, RSW, RW
LF	
R	*IAR* 1962-3, 70 Makkhan Lal 1984, 50 Paul 1985, 86 Ghosh 1989, vol. 2, 392
N	

193. Sapai	
L	
T	
C	PGW cult., NBPW cult., Early Historical P.
D	Sherds: PGW, NBPW, RSW
LF	
R	Makkhan Lal 1984, 50
N	

194. Sarigang	
L	
T	
C	PGW cult., NBPW cult., Early Historical P.
D	Sherds: PGW, NBPW, RSW

LF	
R	Makkhan Lal 1984, 50
N	

195. Sasaimaua	
L	Central part of Kanpur city
T	
C	Twelfth century AD
D	Remains not described
LF	
R	Paul 1985, 87-8
N	Site identified with Sisamau, mentioned in Chhatarpur copper plate (AD 1120)

196. Seng	
L	
T	
C	PGW cult., NBPW cult., Early Historical P.
D	Sherds: PGW, NBPW, RSW
LF	
R	Makkhan Lal 1984, 50
N	

197. Sen-Pachimpur	
L	18 km south of Kanpur
T	Mound

C	Eighth-ninth century AD
D	Sherds: GW, RW Hindu stone sculptures Brickbats Architectural members
LF	
R	Paul 1985, 87
N	Mound locally called Garhi

198. Sheikpur	
L	
T	
C	Late Historical P.
D	Pedestal of Jaina image Architectural members
LF	
R	*IAR* 1976-7, 81
N	

199. Sheoli	
L	16 km south-east of Sheorajpur Mound 1, behind Police station Mound 2, south-west of village
T	Mounds (two)
C	Undated
D	• Mound 1: Traces of bastions • Mound 2:

	Sherds: RW Terracotta animal figurine
LF	
R	Paul 1985, 87
N	

200. Sheorajpur	
L	26°41′ N, 80°9′ E; 33 km north-west of Kanpur
T	
C	Undated
D	3 archaic copper antropomorphic figures
LF	
R	Paul 1985, 87 Ghosh 1989, vol. 2, 407
N	Village founded by Sheorajdeva (AD 1336) (?)

201. Siddhapur Sheoli	
L	
T	
C	PGW cult., NBPW cult., Early Historical P.
D	Sherds: PGW, NBPW, RSW
LF	
R	Makkhan Lal 1984, 50
N	

202. Sultanpur	
L	*Tahsil* Bhoganipur
T	
C	Late Historical P.
D	Sherds: BSW, RW
LF	
R	*IAR* 1992-3, 94-5
N	Sherds picked up from a site called: Paharua baba ki dandi

203. Tegaine	
L	
T	
C	NBPW cult., Early Historical P.
D	Sherds: NBPW, RSW
LF	
R	Makkhan Lal 1984, 50
N	

204. Terhwa	
L	
T	
C	Early Historical P.
D	Sherds: NBPW, RSW
LF	

R	Makkhan Lal 1984, 50
N	

205. Tora	
L	
T	
C	PGW cult., NBPW cult., Early Historical P.
D	Sherds: PGW, NBPW, RSW
LF	
R	Makkhan Lal 1984, 50
N	

206. Turraya	
L	
T	
C	NBPW cult., Early Historical P.
D	Sherds: NBPW, RSW
LF	
R	Makkhan Lal 1984, 50
N	

207. Udaipur	
L	
T	
C	NBPW cult., Early Historical P.
D	Sherds: NBPW, RSW

LF	
R	Makkhan Lal 1984, 50
N	There is a second Udaipur without NBPW cult.

208. Ujjhan or Ujhan	
L	15 km west of Sheoli
T	Mound
C	PGW cult., NBPW cult.
D	Sherds: PGW, NBPW, BPW, RW Terracotta seal with *brahmi* inscription (third-second century BC)
LF	
R	*IAR* 1957-8, 69 *IAR* 1976-7, 53 Paul 1985, 88 Ghosh 1989, vol. 2, 447
N	

209. Umaragarh	
L	
T	
C	NBPW cult.
D	Sherds
LF	
R	*IAR* 1957-8, 69 Ghosh 1989, vol. 2, 450
N	

210. Umaran	
L	
T	
C	NBPW cult., Early Historical P.
D	Sherds: NBPW, RSW
LF	
R	Makkhan Lal 1984, 50
N	

211. Uttha	
L	
T	
C	PGW cult, Early Historical P.
D	Sherds: GW, NBPW, RSW
LF	
R	Makkhan Lal 1984, 50
N	

212. Valmiki Ashram	
L	
T	
C	NBPW cult., Early Historical P.
D	Sherds: NBPW, RSW
LF	

R	*IAR* 1965-6, 48 Makkhan Lal 1984, 50 Ghosh 1989, vol. 2, 459
N	

213. Venda	
L	
T	
C	Late Historical P.
D	Hindu sculptures
LF	
R	*IAR* 1968-9, 39
N	

MAINPURI DISTRICT

53 Sites

1. Aong	
L	
T	
C	PGW cult., NBPW cult.
D	Sherds
LF	
R	*IAR* 1961-2, 57 Tripathi 1976, 124 Shrimali 1983, vol. I, 195 Roy 1986, xxxv Ghosh 1989, vol. 2, 21
N	

2. Aronj	
L	
T	
C	PGW cult., NBPW cult., Late Historical P.
D	Sherds: PGW, NBPW, BSW, RW
LF	
R	*IAR* 1977-8, 58
N	

3. Arsara	
L	
T	
C	PGW cult., NBPW cult., Early Historical P., Late Historical P.
D	Sherds: PGW, NBPW, BSW, RW Terracottas (Sunga-Kushan) 2 copper coins (Kshatrapa, Kushan)
LF	
R	*IAR* 1977-8, 58
N	

4. Behsi̐	
L	
T	
C	PGW cult., NBPW cult., Late Historical P.
D	Sherds: PGW, NBPW, BSW, RW Coins (Kshatrapa, Agnimitra, Muslim)
LF	
R	*IAR* 1977-8, 58
N	

5. Bhagner	
L	
T	
C	PGW cult., NBPW cult., Late Historical P.
D	Sherds: GW, NBPW, BSW, RW

LF	
R	*IAR* 1977-8, 58
N	

6. Bhanwaṭ or Bhanwant	
L	
T	
C	PGW cult., NBPW cult.
D	Sherds: PGW, NBPW, BRW
LF	
R	*IAR* 1961-2, 57 *IAR* 1970-1, 70 Tripathi 1976, 125 Shrimali 1983, vol. I, 196 Roy 1986, xxxv Ghosh 1989, vol. 2, 66
N	

7. Dalippur Sathani	
L	Mound near the railway track
T	Mound
C	PGW cult., NBPW cult., Early Historical P., Late Historical P.
D	Sherds: PGW, NBPW, RW 5 medieval Hindu stone sculptures
LF	
R	*IAR* 1971-2, 80 Ghosh 1989, vol. 2, 115
N	

8. Eka	
L	27°23′04″ N, 78°36′09″ E; 7 km south of Uresar
T	Mound: *c.* 6 ha, *c.* 2 m high
C	PGW cult., NBPW cult., Late Historical P.
D	Sherds: PGW, NBPW, BRW, BSW, RW
LF	
R	*IAR* 1977-8, 58 Chakrabarti et al. 2002, 116
N	

9. Ginoli	
L	
T	
C	PGW cult.
D	Sherds
LF	
R	*IAR* 1960-1, 67 Tripathi 1976, 126 Shrimali 1983, vol. I, 197 Ghosh 1989, vol. 2, 151
N	

10. Ilahabas	
L	
T	
C	PGW cult., NBPW cult.

D	Sherds
LF	
R	*IAR* 1961-2, 57 Tripathi 1976, 126 Ghosh 1989, vol. 2, 172
N	

11. Isai-Khas	
L	
T	
C	PGW cult.
D	Sherds
LF	
R	*IAR* 1961-2, 57 Tripathi 1976, 126 Shrimali 1983, vol. I, 198 Ghosh 1989, vol. 2, 176
N	

12. Itoura	
L	
T	
C	PGW cult., NBPW cult., Late Historical P.
D	Sherds: PGW, NBPW, BSW, RW
LF	
R	*IAR* 1977-8, 58
N	

13. Kalai	
L	
T	
C	PGW cult., NBPW cult.
D	Sherds
LF	
R	*IAR* 1960-1, 67 Tripathi 1976, 127 Shrimali 1983, vol. I, 198 Ghosh 1989, vol. 2, 193
N	

14. Katana	
L	27°23′49″ N, 78°33′25″ E, 5 km west of Eka
T	Mound: *c.* 12 ha
C	Early century AD
D	Finds not described
LF	
R	Chakrabarti et al. 2002, 116
N	

15. Kaurara Buzurg	
L	
T	
C	PGW cult., NBPW cult.
D	Sherds

LF	
R	*IAR* 1961-2, 57 Tripathi 1976, 127 Shrimali 1983, vol. I, 198 Roy 1986, xxxv Ghosh 1989, vol. 2, 211
N	

16. Khariad	
L	
T	
C	PGW cult., NBPW cult., Early Historical P., Late Historical P.
D	Sherds: PGW, NBPW, BSW, RW Terracottas (Sunga-Kushan)
LF	
R	*IAR* 1977-8, 58
N	

17. Khindwari	
L	
T	
C	PGW cult.
D	Sherds
LF	
R	Shrimali 1983, vol. I, 199
N	

18. Kisroam	
L	
T	
C	PGW cult., NBPW cult., Early Historical P., Late Historical P.
D	Sherds: PGW, NBPW, BSW, RW Terracottas (Sunga-Kushan, Gupta)
LF	
R	*IAR* 1977-8, 58
N	

19. Kodar	
L	
T	
C	PGW cult., NBPW cult.
D	Sherds
LF	
R	*IAR* 1960-1, 67 *IAR* 1961-2, 57 Tripathi 1976, 128 Shrimali 1983, vol. I, 199 Roy 1986, xxxv Ghosh 1989, vol. 2, 230
N	

20. Kondra	
L	27°25′46″ N, 78°30′23″ E, 2 km east of Awagarh
T	Mound: *c.* 20 acres

C	PGW cult.
D	Finds not described
LF	
R	Chakrabarti et al. 2002, 116
N	

21. Kushmri

L	
T	
C	PGW cult., NBPW cult., Early Historical P., Late Historical P.
D	Sherds: PGW, NBPW, GW, BSW, BPW, RW Terracottas (Sunga-Kushan, Gupta)
LF	
R	*IAR* 1980-1, 71
N	

22. Kusyami or Kusyani

L	
T	
C	PGW cult.
D	Sherds
LF	
R	*IAR* 1960-1, 67 Tripathi 1976, 128 Shrimali 1983, vol. I, 199 Ghosh 1989, vol. 2, 247
N	

23. Lakshnai	
L	
T	
C	PGW cult.
D	Sherds
LF	
R	*IAR* 1961-2, 57 Tripathi 1976, 128 Shrimali 1983, vol. I, 199 Ghosh 1989, vol. 2, 250
N	

24. Mainpuri	
L	
T	
C	Late Historical P.
D	6 copper rings (Copper Hoard ?) Hindu sculptures
LF	Sculptures collected in Devi temple
R	*IAR* 1968-9, 70 Ghosh 1989, vol. 2, 270
N	

25. Mandai	
L	
T	
C	PGW cult., NBPW cult.

D	Sherds
LF	
R	*IAR* 1961-2, 57 Tripathi 1976, 128 Shrimali 1983, vol. I, 199 Roy 1986, xxxv Ghosh 1989, vol. 2, 275
N	

26. Mehrabad	
L	
T	
C	PGW cult., NBPW cult., Late Historical P.
D	Sherds: PGW, NBPW, BSW, RW
LF	
R	*IAR* 1977-8, 58
N	

27. Nagla Dayal or Nagla Deyal	
L	
T	
C	PGW cult., NBPW cult., Early Historical P., Late Historical P.
D	Sherds: PGW, NBPW, GW, BSW, BPW, RW Terracottas (Sunga-Kushan, Gupta)
LF	

R	*IAR* 1980-1, 71 *IAR* 1981-2, 103
N	

28. Nagla Havelia	
L	
T	
C	PGW cult., NBPW cult., Early Historical P., Late Historical P.
D	Sherds: PGW, NBPW, BRW, BSW, RW
LF	
R	*IAR* 1977-8, 58
N	

29. Nagla Khas Gloura	
L	
T	
C	PGW cult., NBPW cult., Early Historical P., Late Historical P.
D	Sherds: PGW, NBPW, BSW, RW Terracottas (Sunga-Kushan)
LF	
R	*IAR* 1977-8, 58
N	

30. Nagla Khera	
L	
T	Mound
C	PGW cult., NBPW cult., Early Historical P., Late Historical P.
D	Sherds: PGW, NBPW, GW, BSW, BPW, RW (Sunga-Kushan) Terracottas (Sunga-Kushan, Gupta)
LF	
R	*IAR* 1980-1, 71 *IAR* 1981-2, 103
N	

31. Niroli or Ninoli	
L	
T	
C	PGW cult., NBPW cult., Early Historical P., Late Historical P.
D	Sherds: PGW, NBPW, GW, BSW, BPW, RW Terracottas (Sunga-Kushan, Gupta)
LF	
R	*IAR* 1980-1, 71 *IAR* 1981-2, 103
N	

32. Paigu	
L	
T	

C	PGW cult.
D	Sherds
LF	
R	*IAR* 1961-2, 57 Tripathi 1976, 129 Shrimali 1983, vol. I, 200 Ghosh 1989, vol. 2, 325
N	

33. Panwah

L	
T	
C	PGW cult.
D	Sherds
LF	
R	*IAR* 1961-2, 57 Tripathi 1976, 129 Shrimali 1983, vol. I, 200
N	

34. Parham or Param

L	27°19′23″ N, 78°39′ E; southern bank of the Arind River
T	Mound: *c.* 40 ha, 18-20 m high
C	PGW cult., NBPW cult., Early century AD
D	Sherds
LF	

R	*IAR* 1961-2, 57 Tripathi 1976, 129 Shrimali 1983, vol. I, 200 Roy 1986, xxxv Ghosh 1989, vol. 2, 333 Chakrabarti et al. 2002, 116
N	

35. Pariar	
L	
T	
C	PGW cult., NBPW cult.
D	Sherds
LF	
R	*IAR* 1961-2, 57 Tripathi 1976, 129 Shrimali 1983, vol. I, 200 Ghosh 1989, vol. 2, 333
N	

36. Patara	
L	
T	
C	PGW cult.
D	Sherds
LF	

R	*IAR* 1960-1, 67 Tripathi 1976, 129 Shrimali 1983, vol. I, 200 Ghosh 1989, vol. 2, 336
N	

37. Pharengi	
L	
T	
C	PGW cult., NBPW cult.
D	Sherds
LF	
R	*IAR* 1961-2, 57 Tripathi 1976, 129 Shrimali 1983, vol. I, 200 Roy 1986, xxxv Ghosh 1989, vol. 2, 342
N	

38. Praonkh	
L	
T	
C	NBPW cult., Early Historical P., Late Historical P.
D	Sherds: NBPW, BSW, RW
LF	
R	*IAR* 1977-8, 58
N	

39. Pundri	
L	
T	
C	PGW cult., NBPW cult., Early Historical P., Late Historical P.
D	Sherds: PGW, NBPW, BSW, RW
LF	
R	*IAR* 1977-8, 58
N	

40. Rasemar	
L	
T	
C	PGW cult.
D	Sherds
LF	
R	*IAR* 1961-2, 57 Tripathi 1976, 129 Shrimali 1983, vol. I, 201 Ghosh 1989, vol. 2, 372
N	

41. Sahan	
L	
T	
C	PGW cult., NBPW cult., Early Historical P., Late Historical P.

D	Sherds: PGW, NBPW, GW, BSW, BPW, RW (Sunga-Kushan) Terracottas (Sunga-Kushan, Gupta)
LF	
R	*IAR* 1977-8, 58 *IAR* 1980-1, 71 *IAR* 1981-2, 103
N	

42. Salempur Perhina	
L	
T	
C	PGW cult., NBPW cult.
D	Sherds
LF	
R	*IAR* 1961-2, 57 Tripathi 1976, 130 Shrimali 1983, vol. I, 201 Roy 1986, xxxv Ghosh 1989, vol. 2, 385
N	

43. Sarai Bharthara	
L	
T	
C	PGW cult., NBPW cult., Early Historical P., Late Historical P.
D	Sherds: PGW, NBPW, BSW, RW

LF	
R	*IAR* 1977-8, 58
N	

44. Shamsherganj-Maholi	
L	
T	
C	PGW cult., NBPW cult.
D	Sherds
LF	
R	*IAR* 1961-2, 57 Tripathi 1976, 130 Shrimali 1983, vol. I, 201 Roy 1986, xxxv Ghosh 1989, vol. 2, 406
N	

45. Sherpur Qutbpur	
L	
T	
C	PGW cult., NBPW cult., Early Historical P., Late Historical P.
D	Sherds: PGW, NBPW, BSW, RW
LF	
R	*IAR* 1977-8, 58
N	

46. Sirsaganj	
L	
T	
C	PGW cult., NBPW cult.
D	Sherds
LF	
R	*IAR* 1961-2, 57 Tripathi 1976, 130 Shrimali 1983, vol. I, 202 Roy 1986, xxxv Ghosh 1989, vol. 2, 412
N	

47. Thorue	
L	27°24′54″ N, 78°31′36″ E; 5 km south-east of Awagarh
T	Mound: *c.* 6 acres, *c.* 5 m high
C	Early century AD
D	Sherds
LF	
R	Chakrabarti et al. 2002, 116
N	

48. Ujjhani or Ujhiani	
L	
T	
C	Late Historical P.

D	Hindu sculptures
LF	
R	*IAR* 1970-1, 70 *IAR* 1977-8, 84
N	

49. Ukhrend	
L	
T	
C	PGW cult.
D	Sherds
LF	
R	*IAR* 1961-2, 57 Tripathi 1976, 131 Shrimali 1983, vol. I, 202 Ghosh 1989, vol. 2, 450
N	

50. Uncha-Islamabad	
L	
T	
C	PGW cult., NBPW cult.
D	Sherds
LF	
R	*IAR* 1961-2, 57 Tripathi 1976, 131 Shrimali 1983, vol. I, 202 Ghosh 1989, vol. 2, 451
N	

51. Uresar	
L	27°25′55″ N, 78°35′37″ E; left bank of the Arind
T	Mound: *c.* 6 m high
C	Late Historical P.
D	Finds not described
LF	
R	Chakrabarti et al. 2002, 116
N	

52. Utrala or Utrara	
L	
T	
C	PGW cult.
D	Sherds
LF	
R	*IAR* 1960-1, 67 Tripathi 1976, 131 Shrimali 1983, vol. I, 202 Ghosh 1989, vol. 2, 454
N	

53. Vinayekpur	
L	
T	
C	Kushan period
D	Hindu sculptures

LF	
R	*IAR* 1977-8, 84
N	

BIBLIOGRAPHIC REFERENCES

AI: Ancient India, New Delhi.

Agrawal, D.P., Chakrabarti, D.K. (eds.), 1979, *Essays in Indian Protohistory*, Delhi: B.R. Publishing Corporation.

BMA: Bulletin of Museums & Archaeology, Lucknow.

Chakrabarti, D.K. 1997, *The Archaeology of Ancient Indian Cities*, Delhi: Oxford University Press.

———, 2001, *Archaeological Geography of the Ganga Plain—The lower and the middle Ganga*, Delhi: Permanent Black.

Chakrabarti, D.K., Tewari, R., 2000, 'Lower Doab and Oudh: Sites between Pratapgarh and Sitapur', *South Asian Studies*, vol. 16, pp. 109-17.

Chakrabarti, D.K., Tewari, R., Singh, R.N., Singh, K.K., Trivedi, R., 2002, 'Kampil Sankisa and Chakranagar: Sites in the Farrukhabad-Etah-Budaun-Mainpuri-Etawah Region of Uttar Pradesh', *South Asian Studies*, vol. 18, pp. 109-19.

Dallaporta, A., Marcato, L. 1999, 'Kampilya: One Site or More Sites?', in G.G. Filippi, B. Marcolongo (eds.), *Kampilya—Quest for a Mahabharata City*, New Delhi: D.K. Printworld, pp. 31-64.

———, 2001, 'Where is Kampilya? Archaeological research in Farrukhabad district', *South Asian Studies*, vol. 17, pp. 161-9.

Dey, N., 1927 (rep. 1979), *The Geographical Dictionary of Ancient and Medieval India*, New Delhi: Cosmo Publications.

Dhavalikar, M.K., 1997, *Indian Protohistory*, New Delhi: Books & Books.

Dikshit, K.N., 1979, 'The Ochre Coloured Ware Settlements in Ganga-Yamuna Doab', in D.P. Agrawal, D.K. Chakrabarti (eds.), *Essays in Indian Protohistory*, Delhi: B.R. Publishing Corporation.

———, 'Report of the First Archaeological Campaign at Drupad Kila (Kampilya)', *Puratattva*, no. 30, pp. 164-72.

Erdösi, G., 1987, 'Early Historic Cities of Northern India', *South Asian Studies*, vol. 3, pp. 1-23.

Ghosh, A. (ed.), 1989, *An Encyclopaedia of Indian Archaeology*, vol. 2, New Delhi: Munshiram Manoharlal.

Gupta, S.P. (ed.), 1995, *The 'lost' Sarasvati and the Indus Civilization*, Jodhpur: Kusumanjali Prakashan.

IAR: Indian Archaeology: a Review, New Delhi.

Makkhan Lal, 1984, *Archaeology of Population*, Monography of the Department of Ancient Indian History, Culture and Archaeology, no. 12, Varanasi.

Paul, R.K., 1985, *South Pancala—A Study in Historical and Cultural Geography*, Kanpur: Sahitya Niketan.

Paul, R.K., 1990, 'Survey Report', *Pancala*, vol. 4, no. 4, Kanpur: Panchal Research Institute.

Possehl, G.L., 1986, *Indian Archaeology, A Review—Guide to excavated sites 1953/54 through 1983/84*, University of Pennsylvania, The University Museum.

Roy, T.N., 1983, *The Ganges Civilization*, New Delhi: Ramanand Vidya Bhavan.

———, 1986, *A Study of Northern Black Polished Ware Culture—An Iron Age Culture of India*, New Delhi: Ramanand Vidya Bhavan.

Shrimali, K.M., 1983, *History of Pancala—to c.* AD *550*, vol. I, New Delhi: Munshiram Manoharlal.

Singh, S.B., 1979, *Archaeology of Pañchàla Region*, Delhi: Agam Kala Prakashan.

———, 1984 ?, 'Archaeology of Ethah District', *Panchal through the ages*, Kanpur: Panchal Research Institute, pp. 1-11.

Shukla, K.S., 1987, 'A pre-Harappan Seal from Indira Nagar Mound (Kanpur)', *Bulletin of Museums & Archaeology*, no. 39, Lucknow, pp. 55-8.

Tripathi, V., 1976, *The Painted Grey Ware—An Iron Age Culture of Northern India*, Delhi: Concept Publishing Company.

INDEX